More praise for **Poli's Dogs**

"Poli's Dogs is a wondrous journey into an artist's love of canine creatures, in particular Poli's own, but with obvious dedication, love and compassion toward all dogs! This sensitive, comical, and joyous romp through the dunes with dogs as subject matter is a great exploration not only of human's love and affection of animals but also the emotional attachment and companionship we have with our pets ... This is a loving and extraordinarily beautiful and timeless book for all those who love animals."
—France Garrido, Director of Hob'art Co-operative Gallery, www.francegarrido.com

"Nicoletta captures through her paintings all the joy and wonder our animals experience in the great outdoors as well as the intimate connection we have to them."
—Richard Knudsen, artist and co-owner of the POLi Gallery, www.rgknudsen.com

"Nicoletta's paintings capture dogs' expressions and personalities, the tilt of an ear, the angle of a tail. These gestures, gone in a second, help us remember the delightful quirkiness of our own dogs. As if this is not enough, the backgrounds of the paintings gorgeously depict the changing light and color through the days and seasons, and transport us to the sea and outdoors."
—Jill Mulholland, artist, Coordinator, International Association of Lighting Designers Education Trust

"Some of my favorite memories in life involve experiences I've had with my dog. Nicoletta's paintings capture the spirit of these wonderful and loyal companions. The vibrant colors of her paintings, the vivid landscapes and the simple lift of the dogs' ears all remind us just why our bond with our pets is so great."
—Kee Kee Buckley, writer, www.seekingshama.com

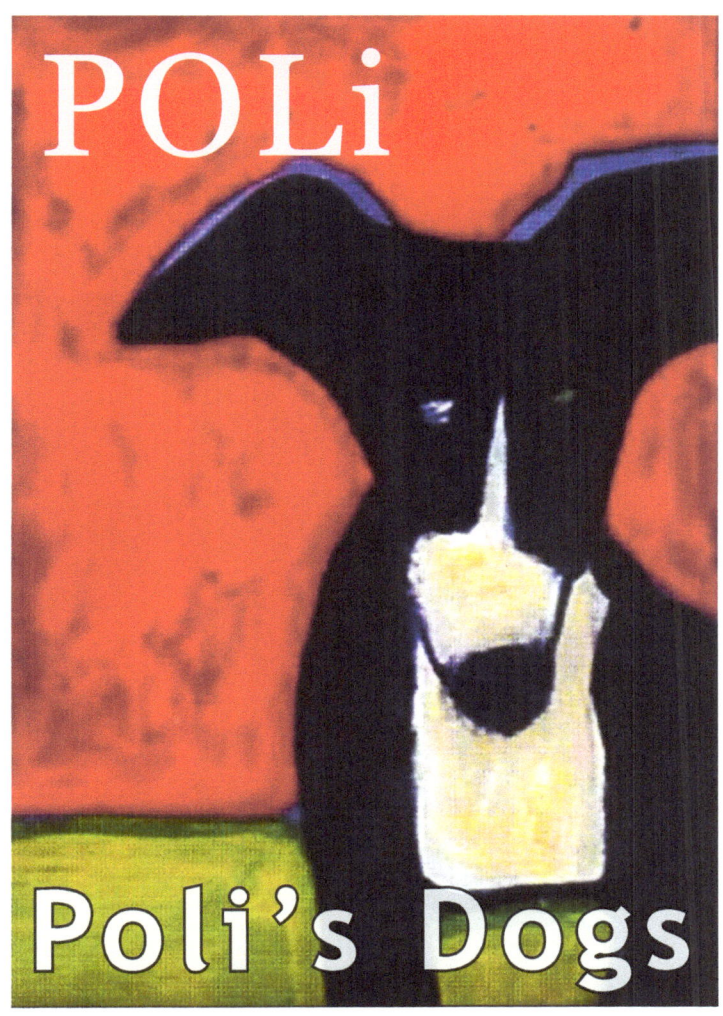

POLi

Poli's Dogs

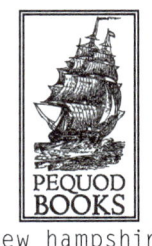

PEQUOD
BOOKS

new hampshire

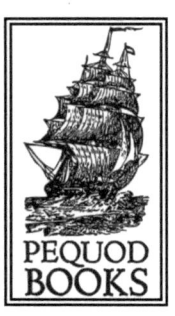

Pequod Books LLC
6 Hudson Hills Drive
Hudson, NH 03061
www.PequodBooks.com

Poli's Dogs

Copyright © 2012 Nicoletta Poli

Book design by Pequod Book Design

All rights reserved.

ISBN-10: 0984785000
ISBN-13: 978-0-9847850-0-1

Visit Pequod Books on the web at www.pequodbooks.com

PRINTED IN THE UNITED STATES OF AMERICA

I would like to dedicate it to my mother, Grace.
Whose love for dogs equals mine.

Introduction by the artist

I've been painting dogs for the last 20 years—primarily mine. They love me, and I love them; that makes them the best subject to paint. Being a painter gives me the advantage of transforming my feelings into color and shape. In this book, I've included my dogs Luna, Pablo, and Mickey as well as my friend Beth and her Golden Retrievers.

A morning walk turns into a tapestry of color, shape and light. Observing my dogs evokes endless possibilities to draw from. Their joy brings infinite amounts of inspiration. Just a simple gesture, the shape of their noses, the white tips of their tails, it all falls into place: dunes, dogs, sea, and sky. It's all so very beautiful to me. In this book, I hope to show you how a simple painting can evoke the greatest of all emotions, the love between humans and dogs.

Poli's Dogs

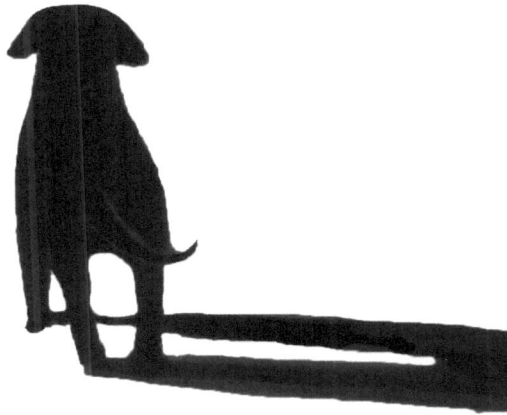

Toss

"Pablo always gets the ball"

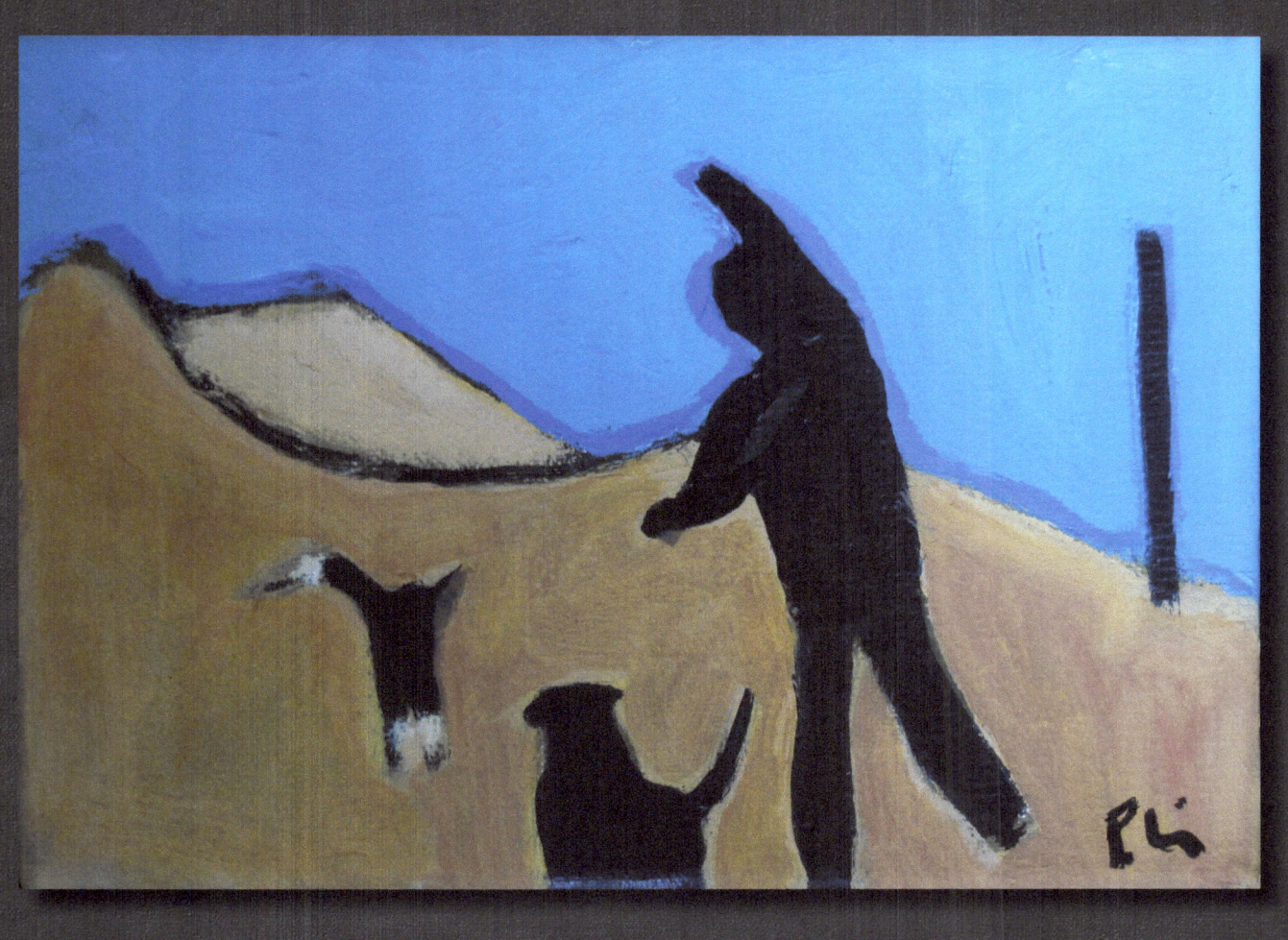

BARK

"Every opportunity he gets."

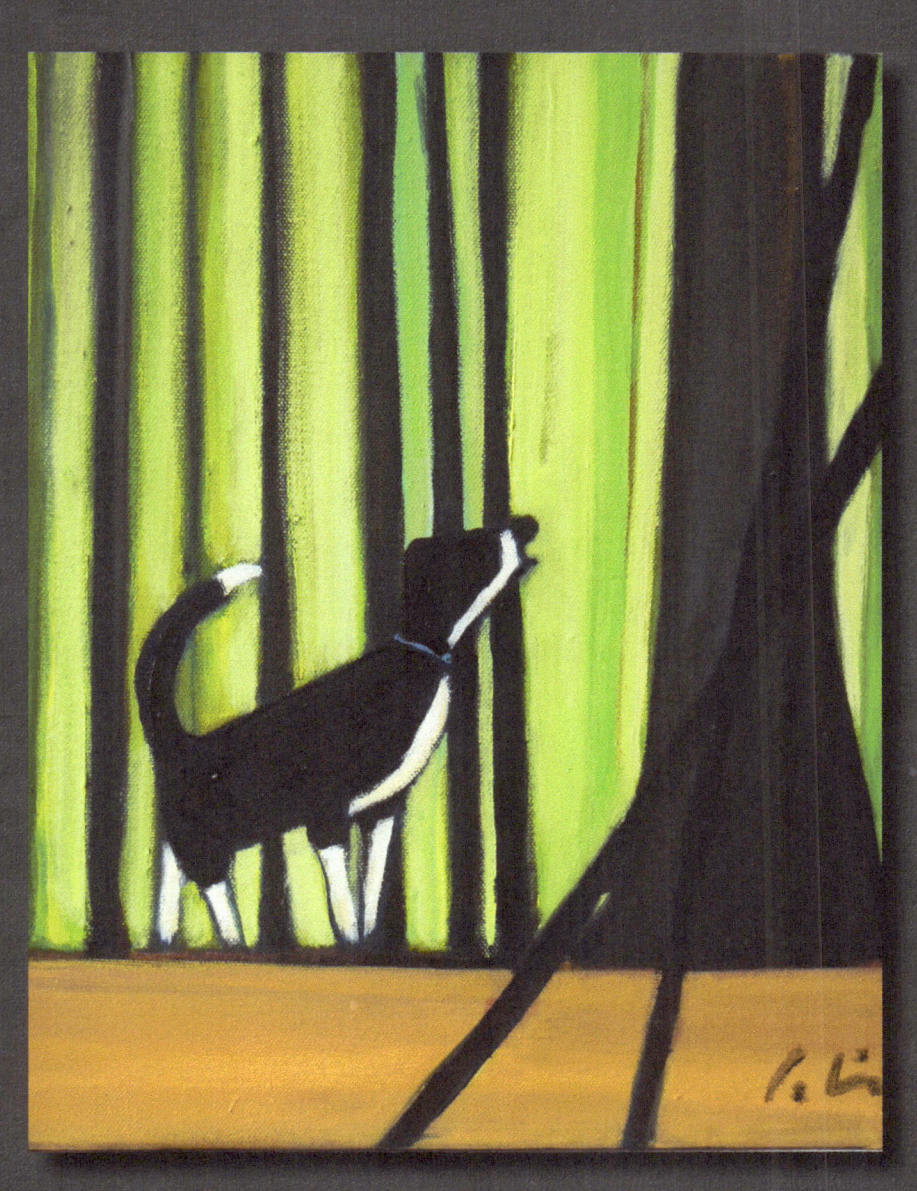

Blacktail

"Mickey showing off his best side"

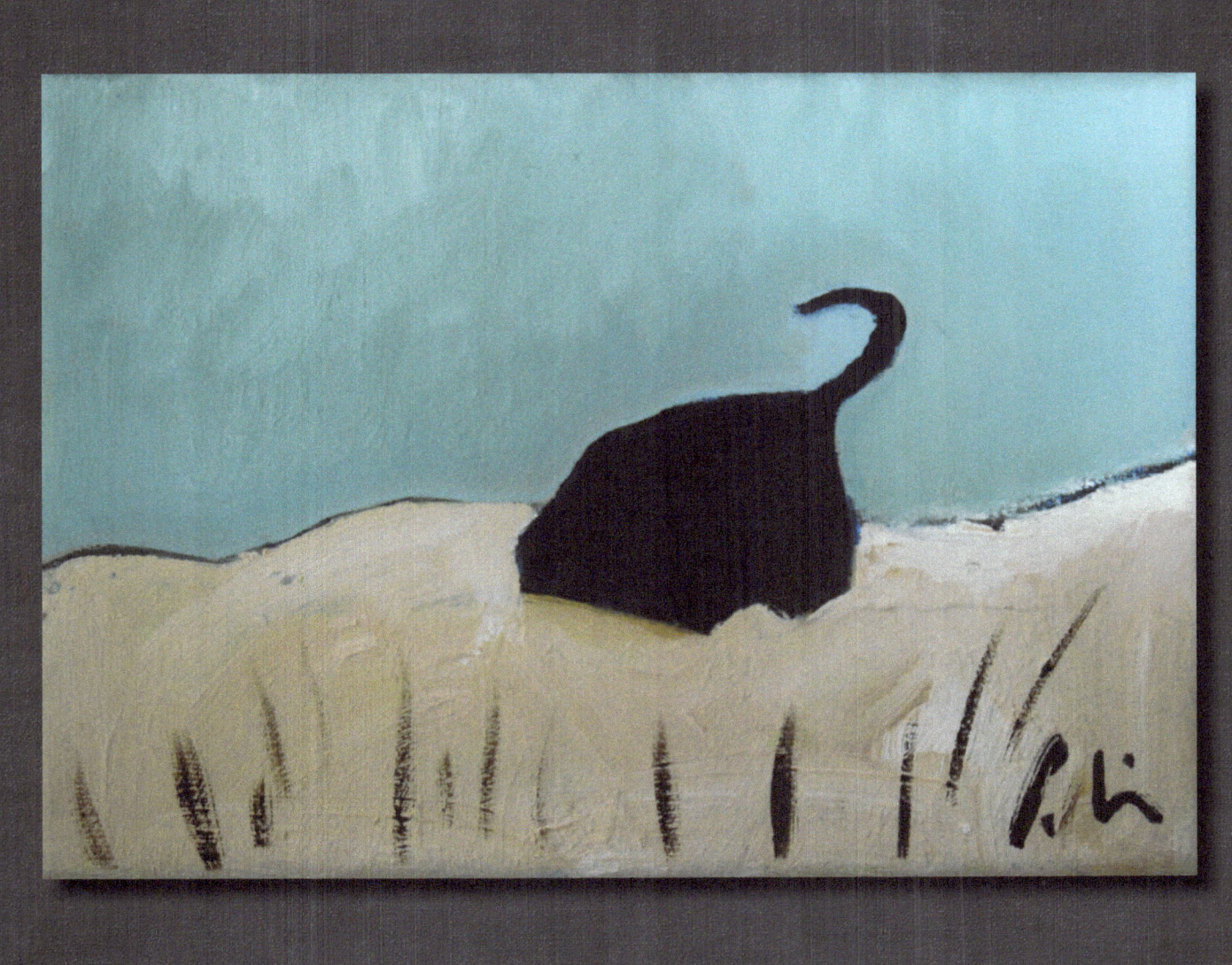

At the Pond

"A true bird dog"

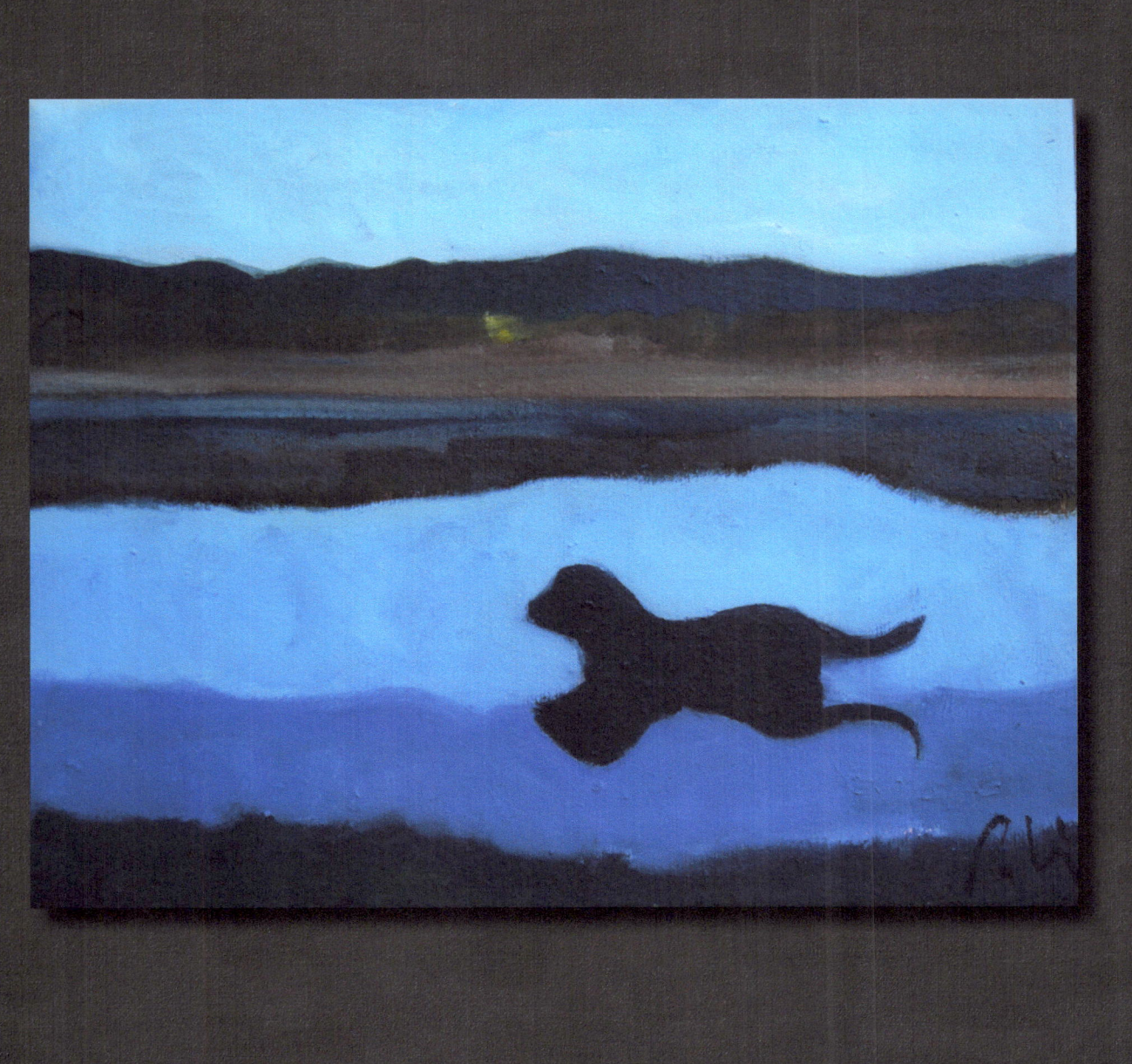

BIG BABY

"The Biggest!"

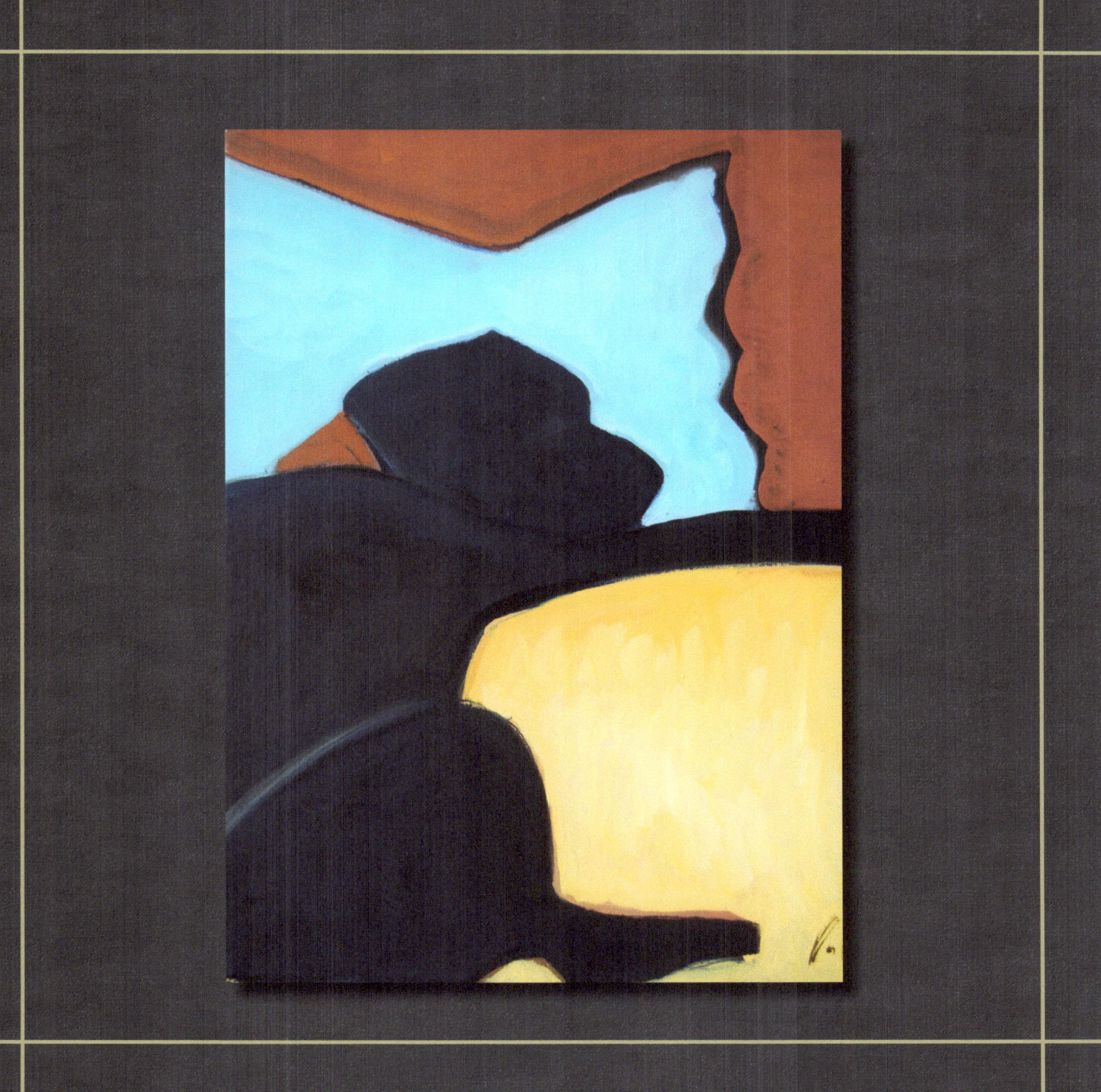

Noses

"Resting on each other"

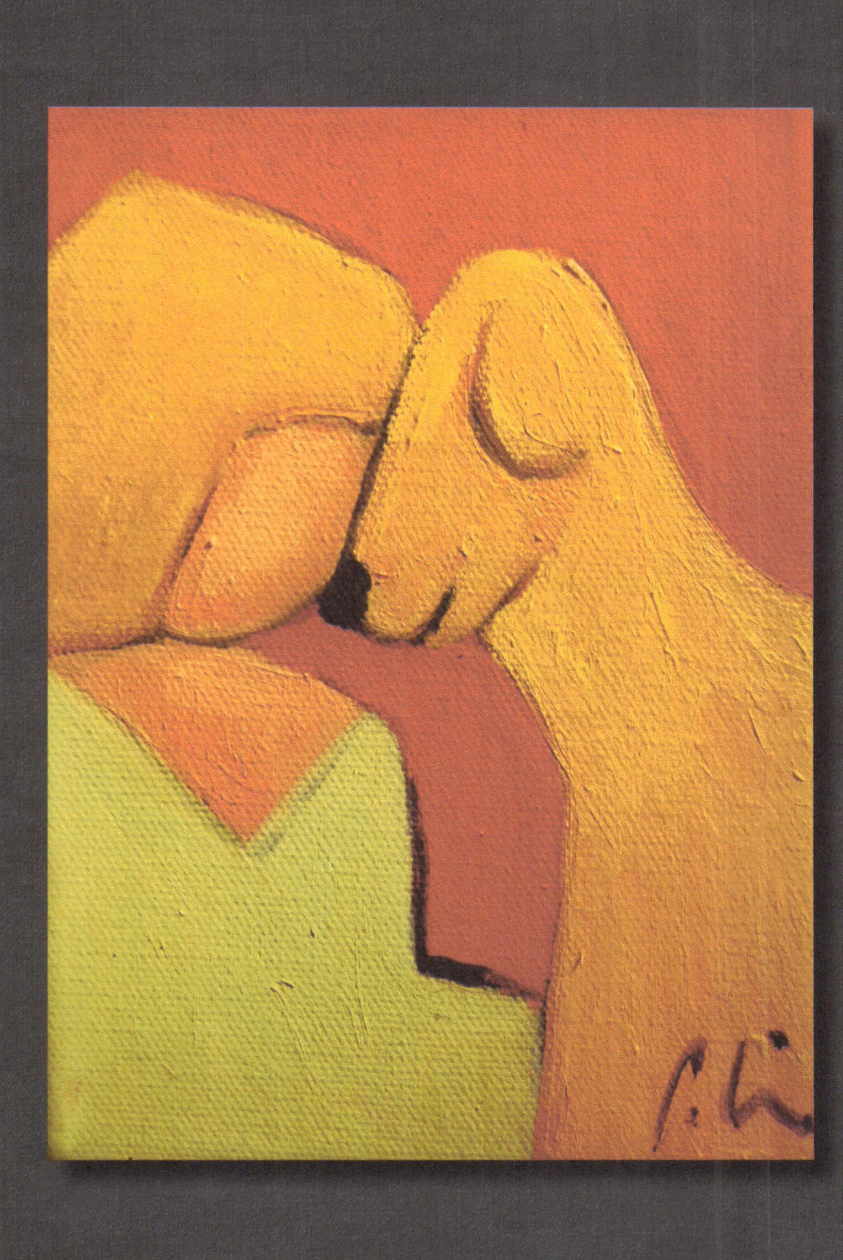

BLUEGRASS

"Pointed ears and pointy nose."

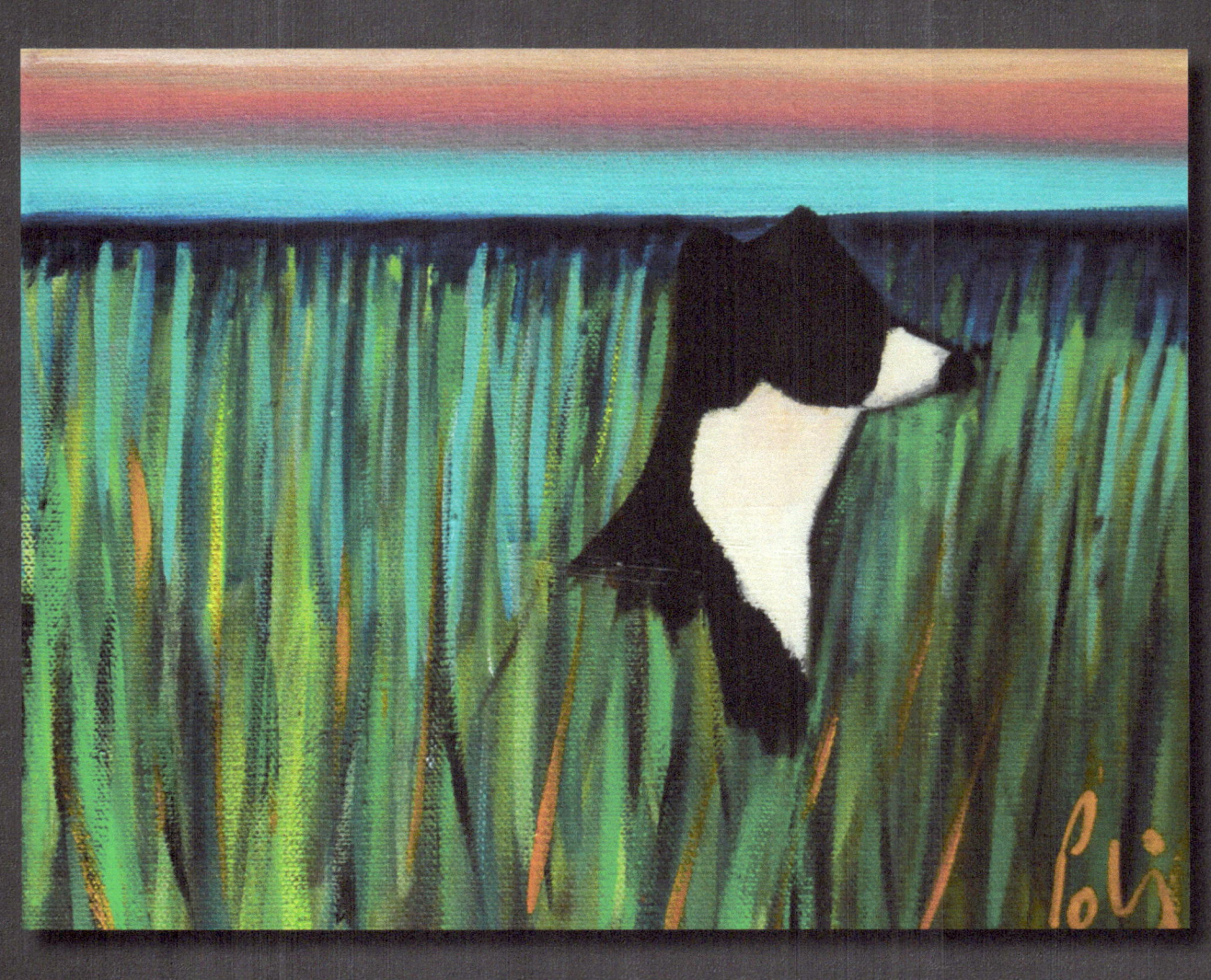

EARLY

"Our favortie time of day for a swim."

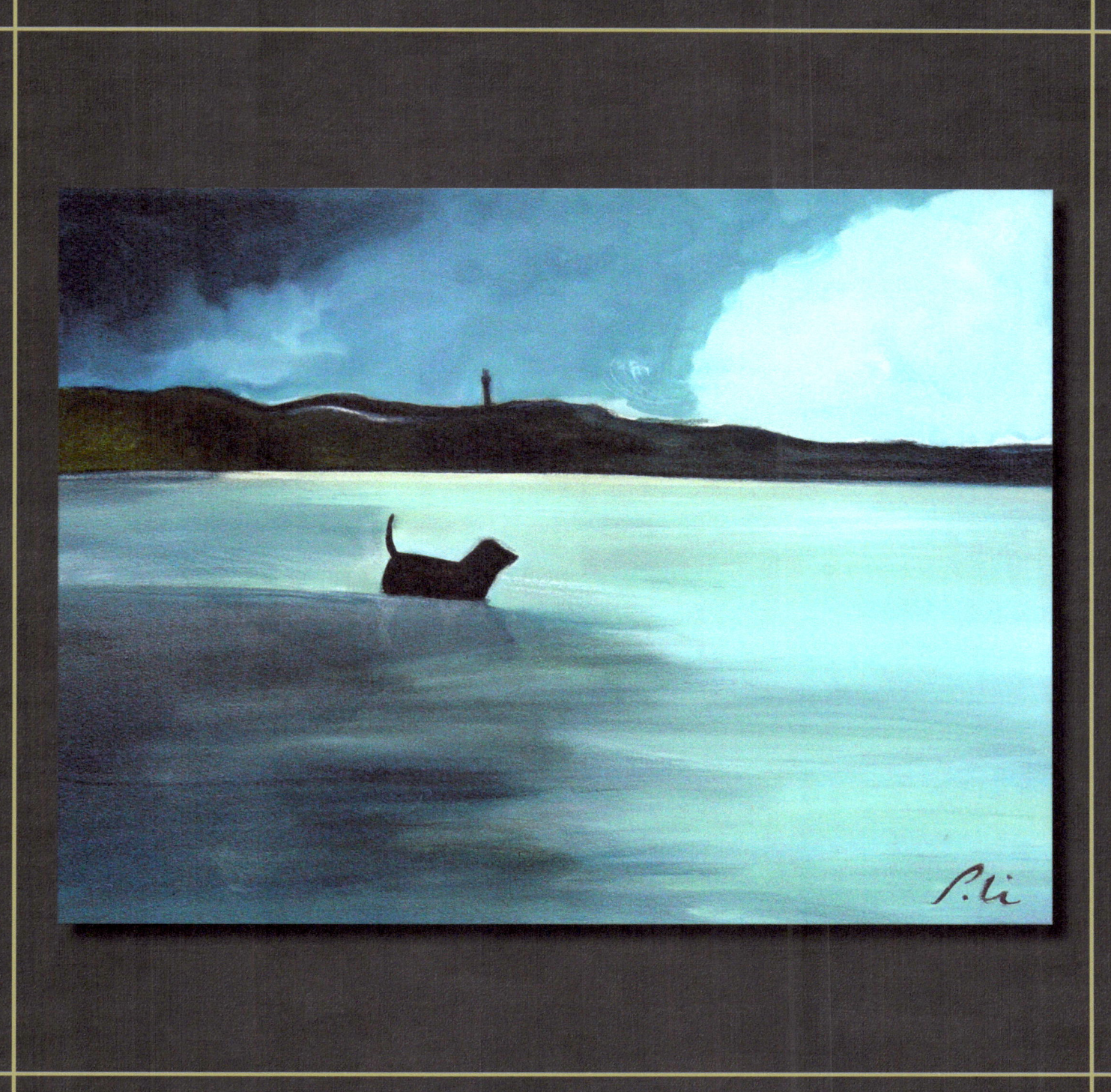

BEAUTIFUL DAY

"Who could ask for more?"

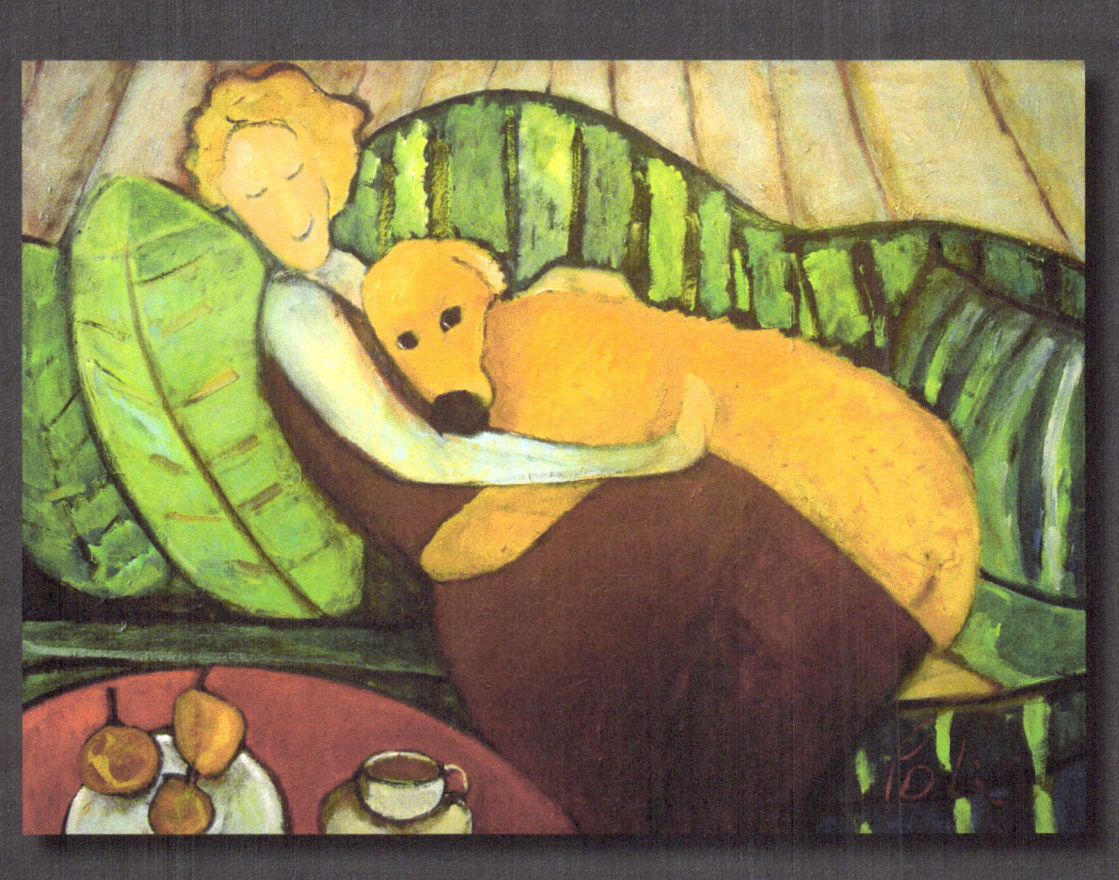

THE MODEL

"The still life always adds to his beauty."

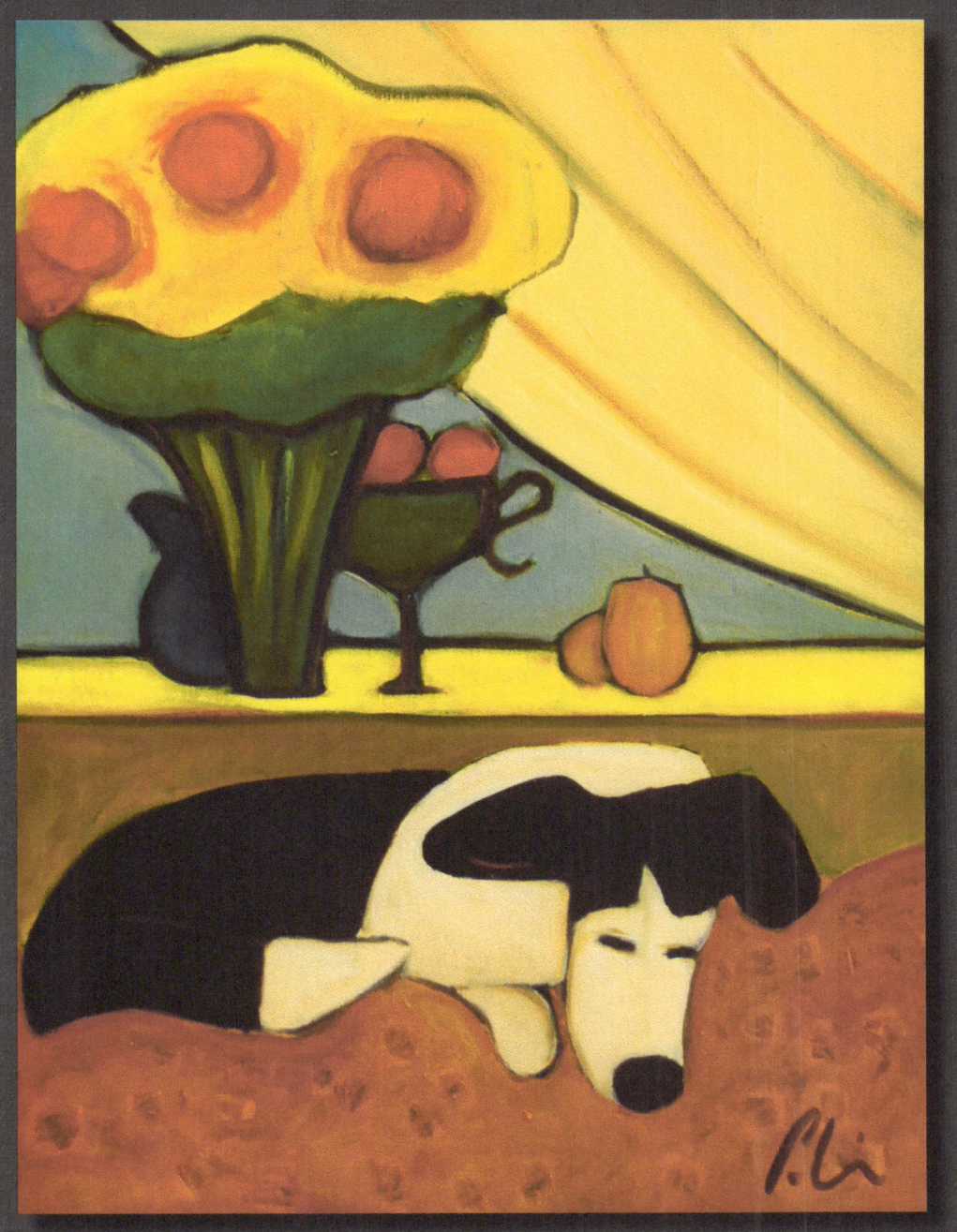

FARTHEST EAST

*"We love living across the street
from this beautiful place."*

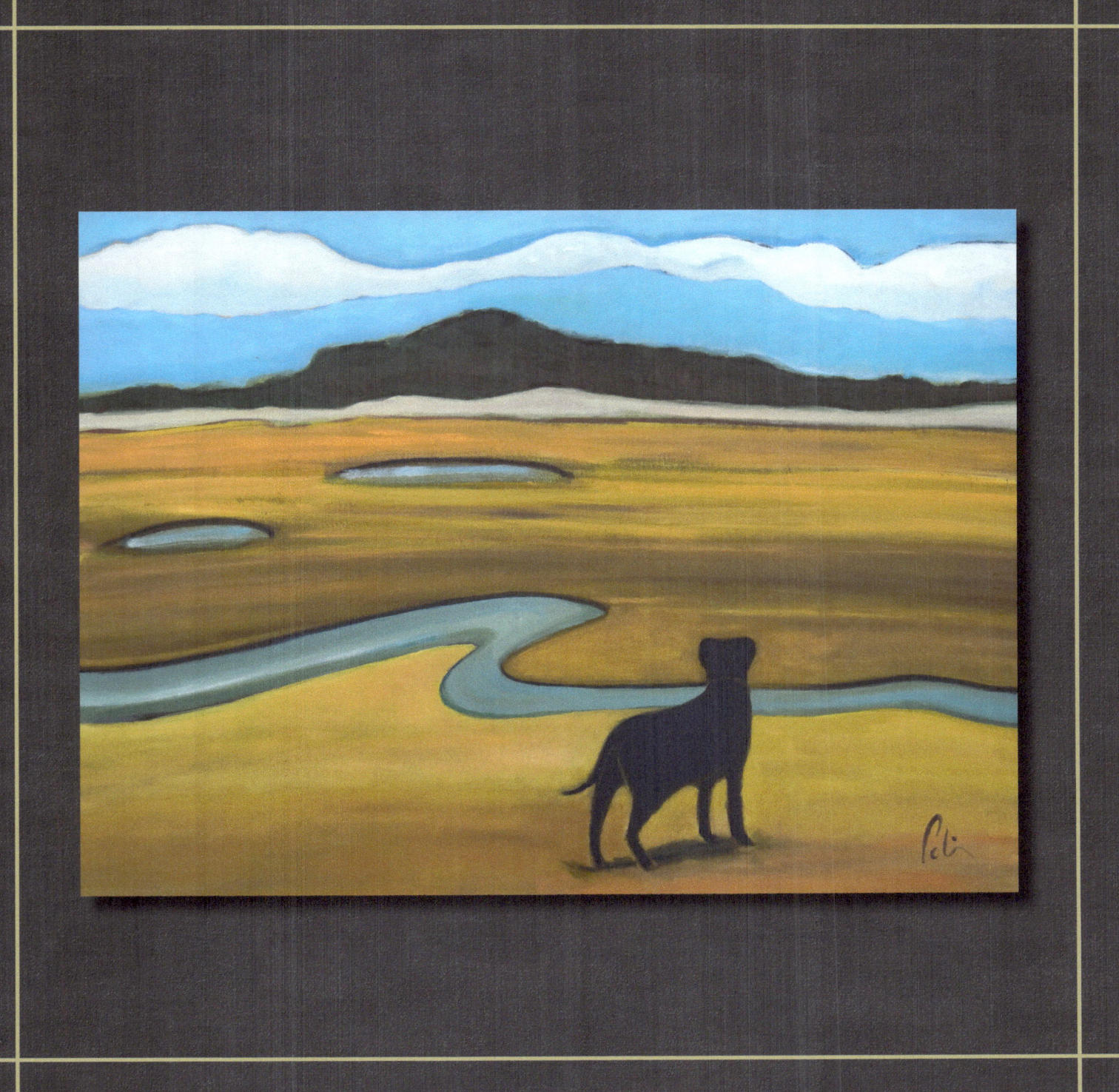

Foggy Morning

*"I love it when the sea and sky blend.
Mickey adds to the mood."*

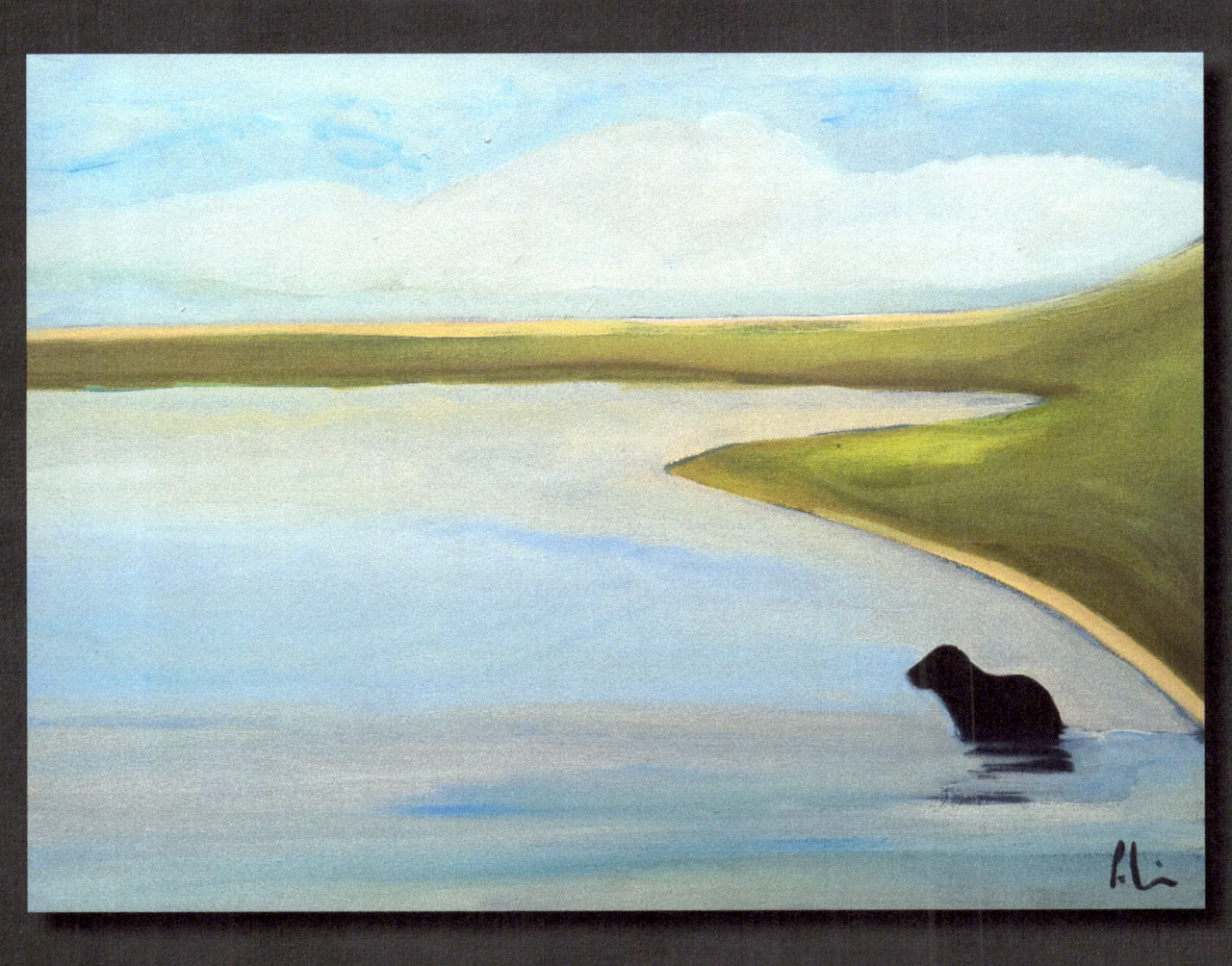

FOREVER

"I wanted to title this painting 'Forever and Ever and Ever'."

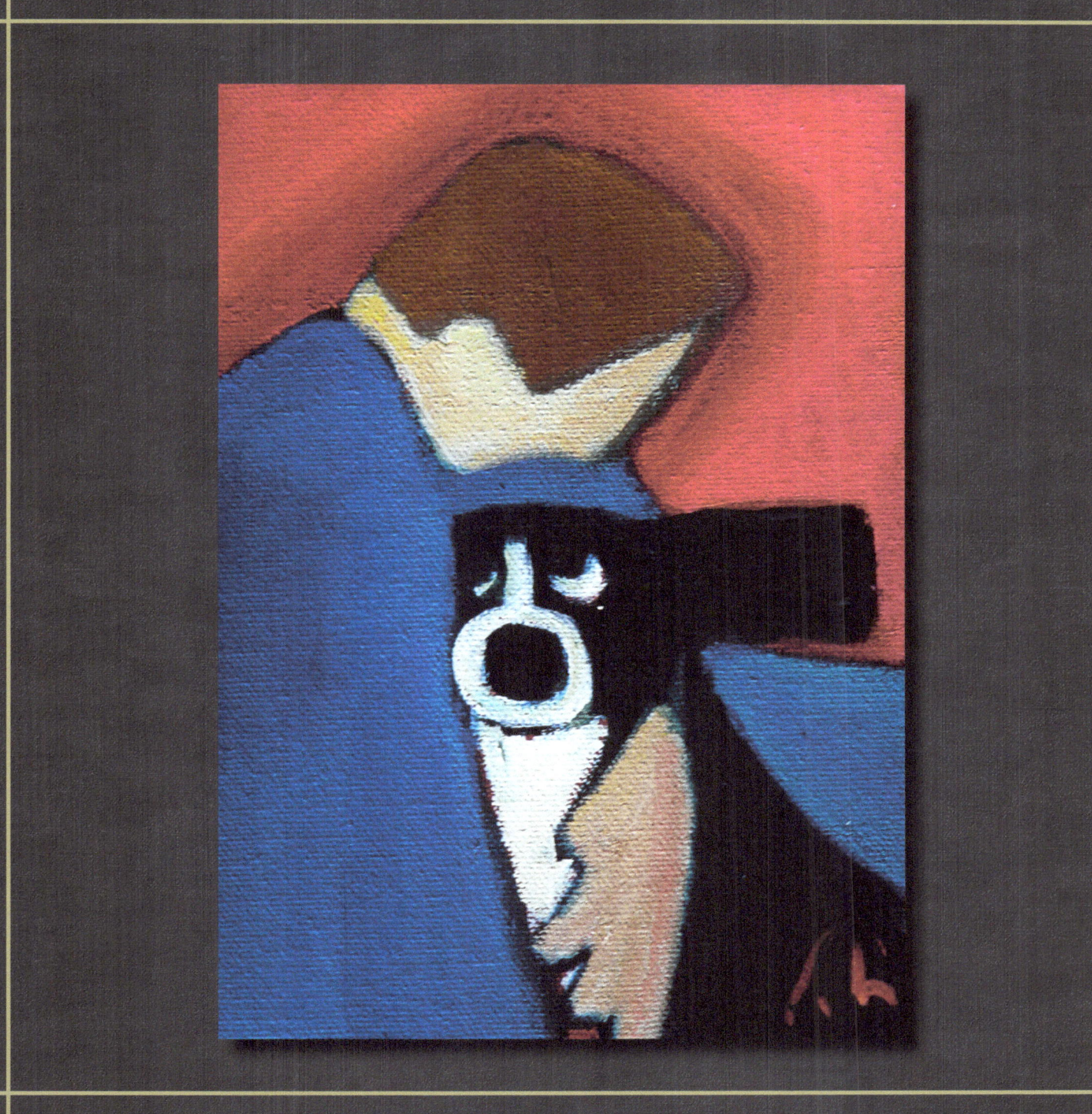

Aunt Beth

"Fighting for position"

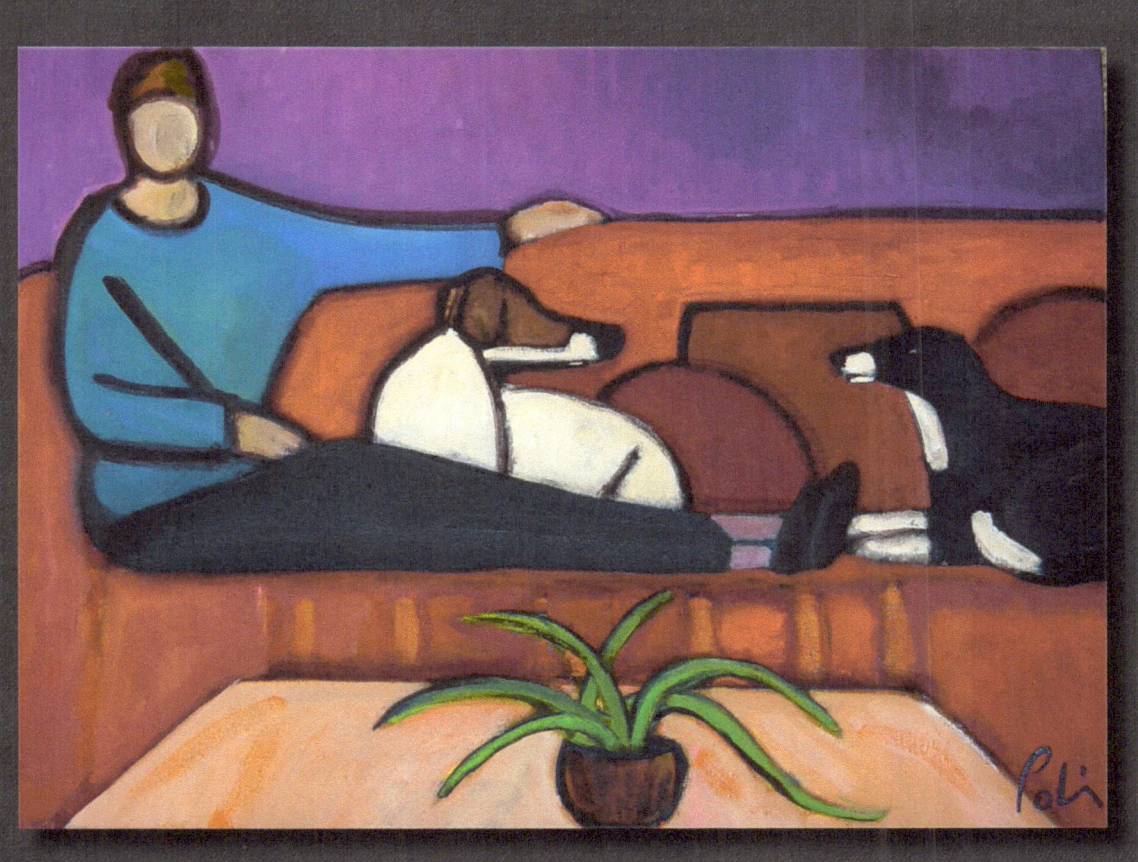

HAPPY FALL DAY

"Everyday is a happy day for this scruffy little boy!"

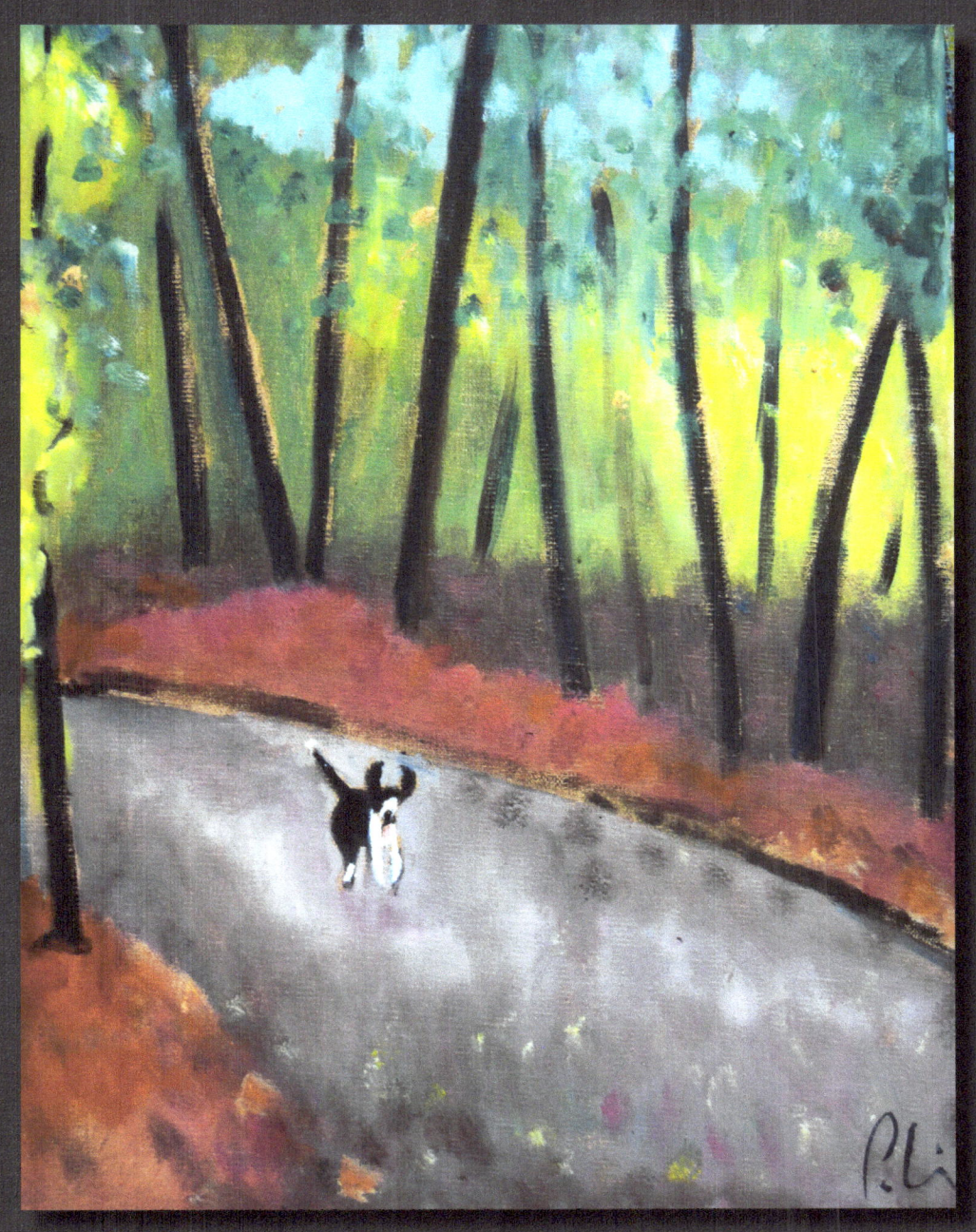

Heaven

"No better place to be."

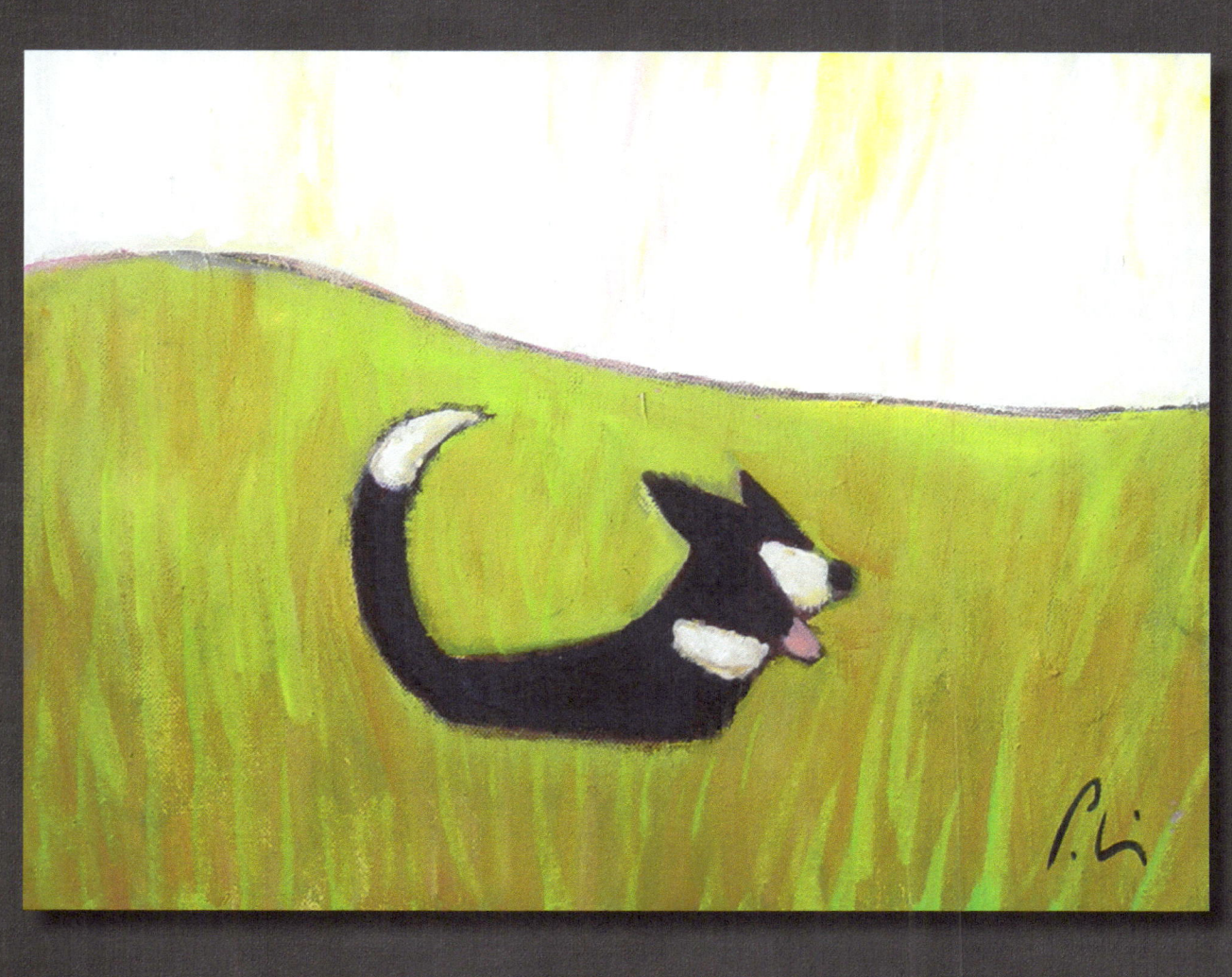

HOME

"Mickey's favorite part of town"

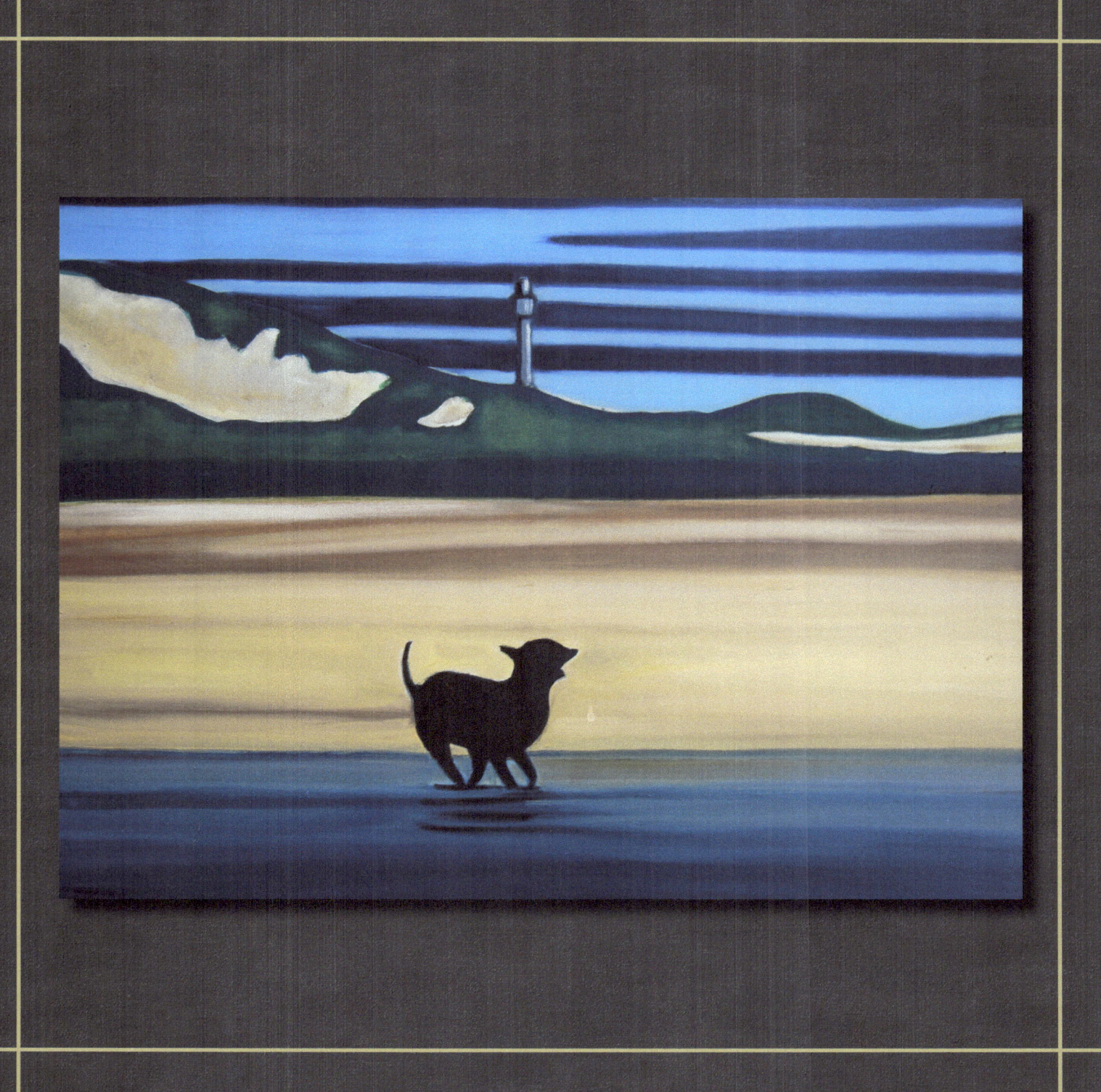

THE FOREST

"Simplifying the moment"

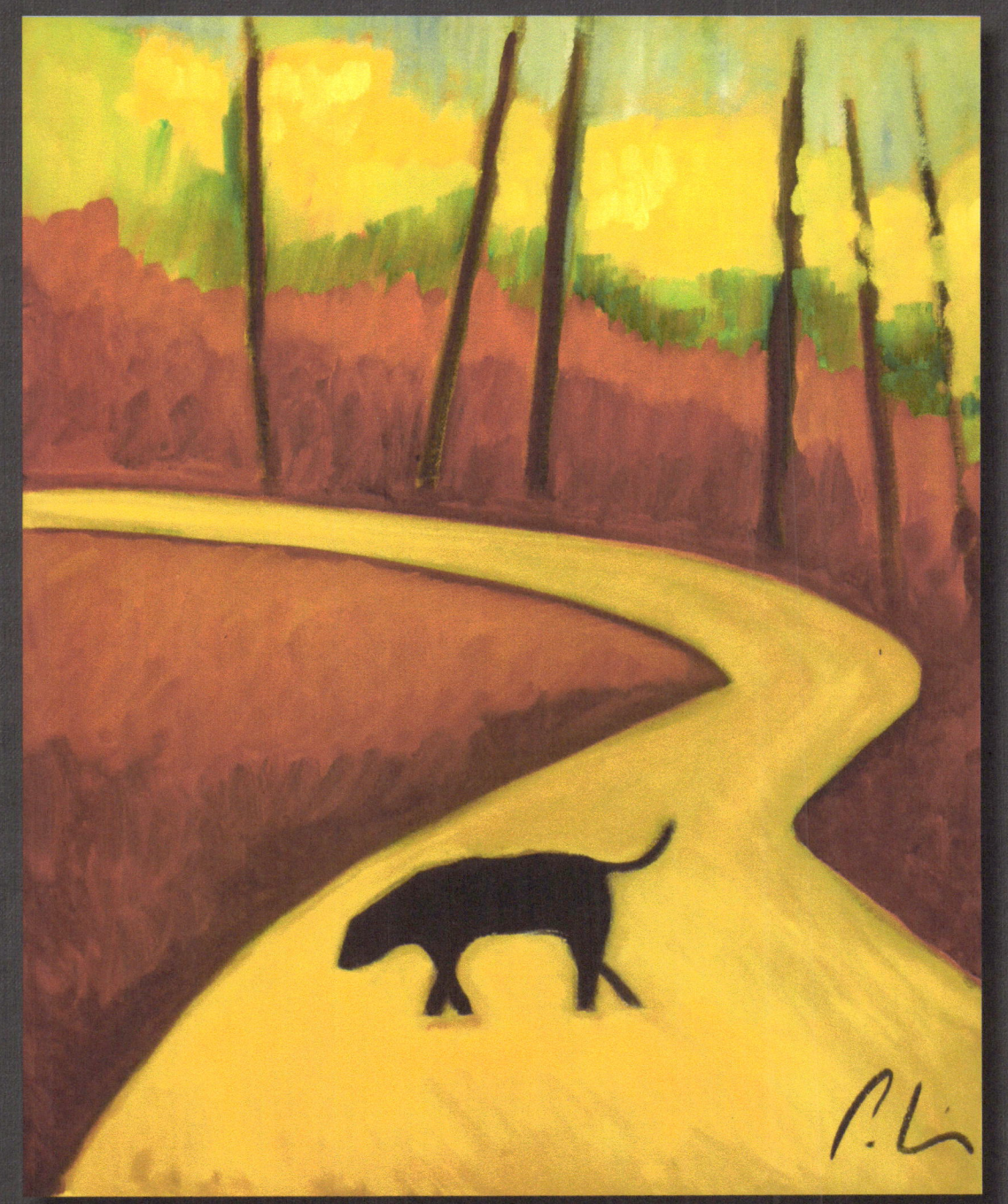

In The Woods

"She thinks she's hiding."

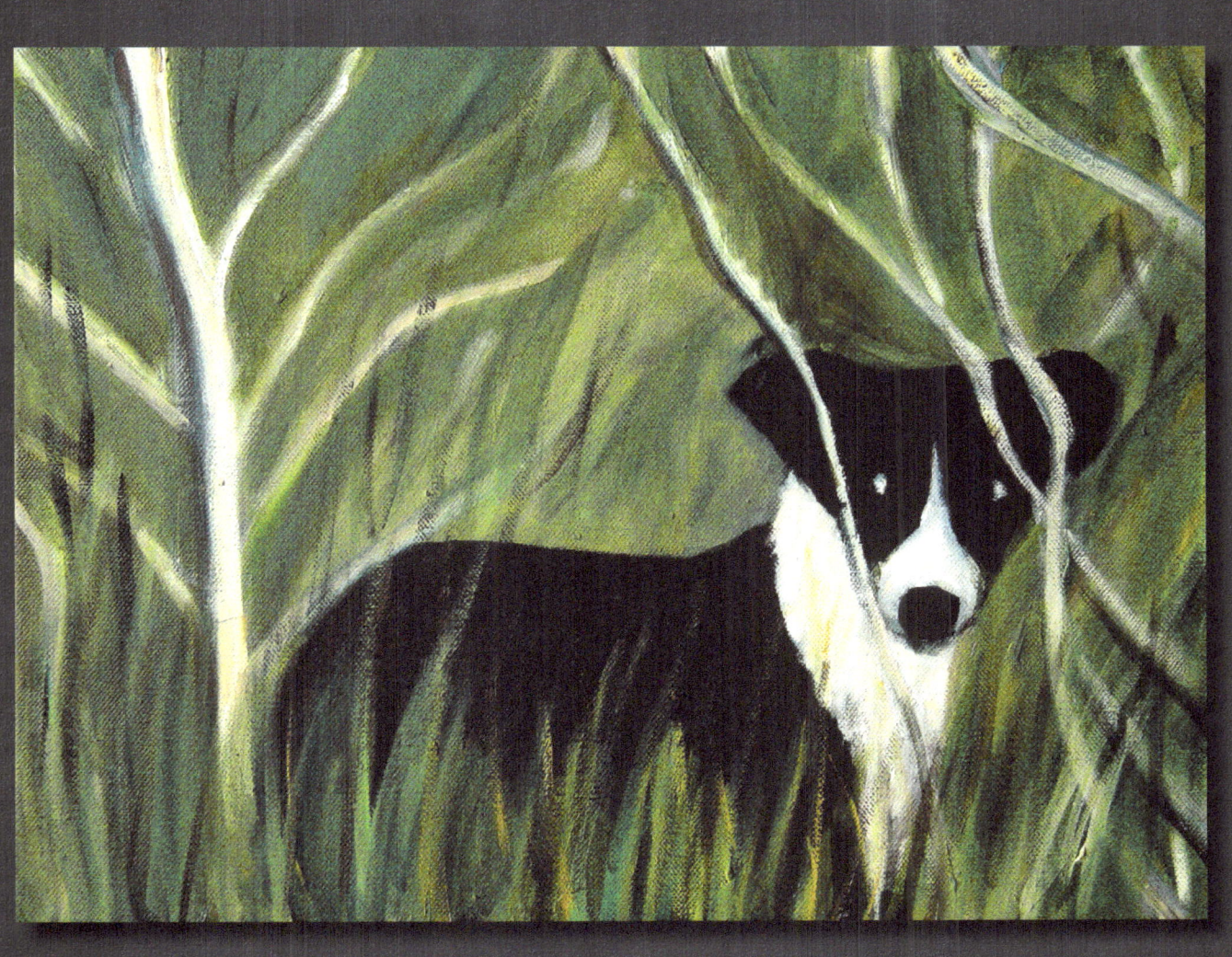

Magical Kingom

"What it must feel for him"

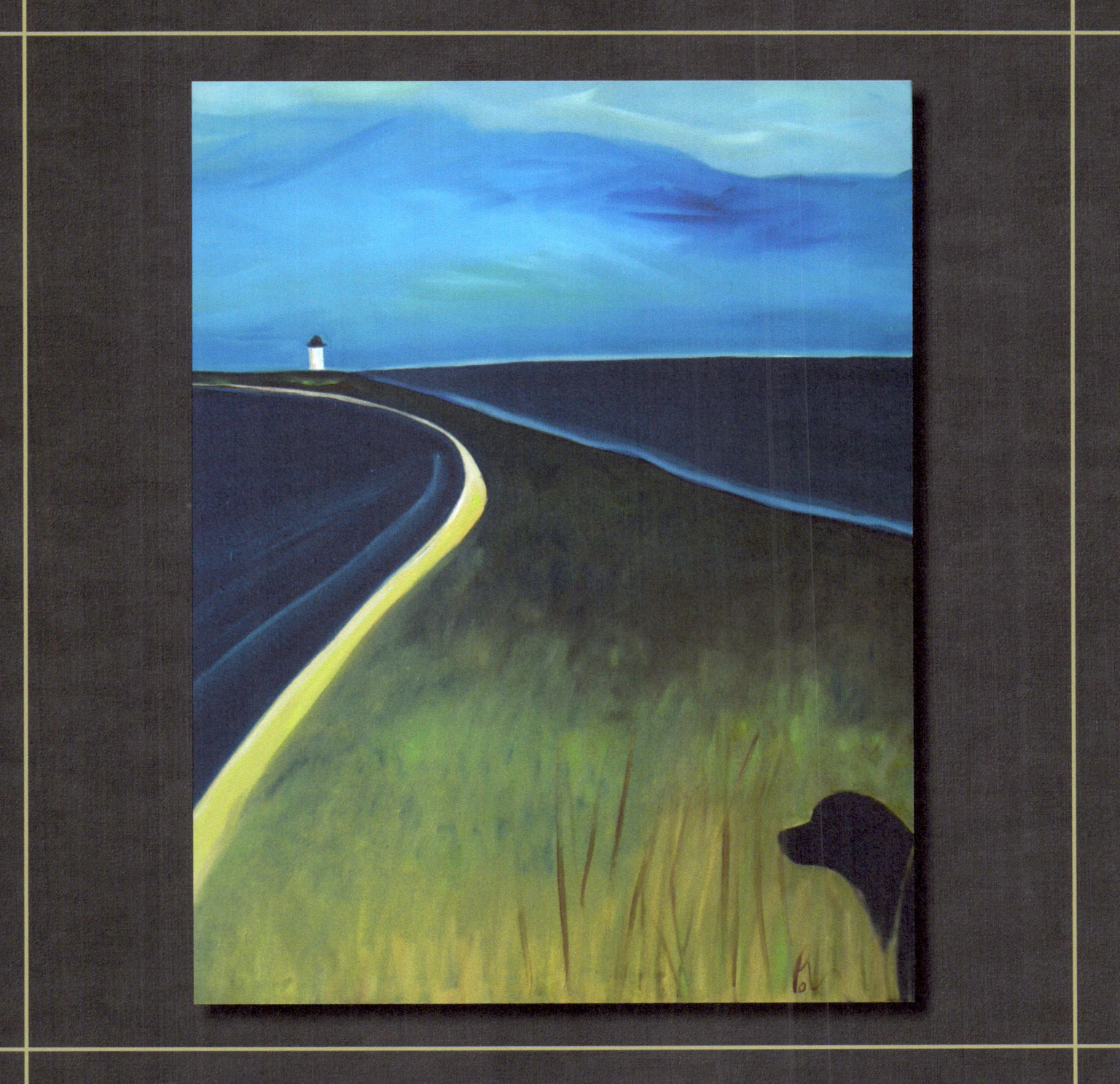

MICKEY AT THE LIGHTHOUSE

"We love living by the water."

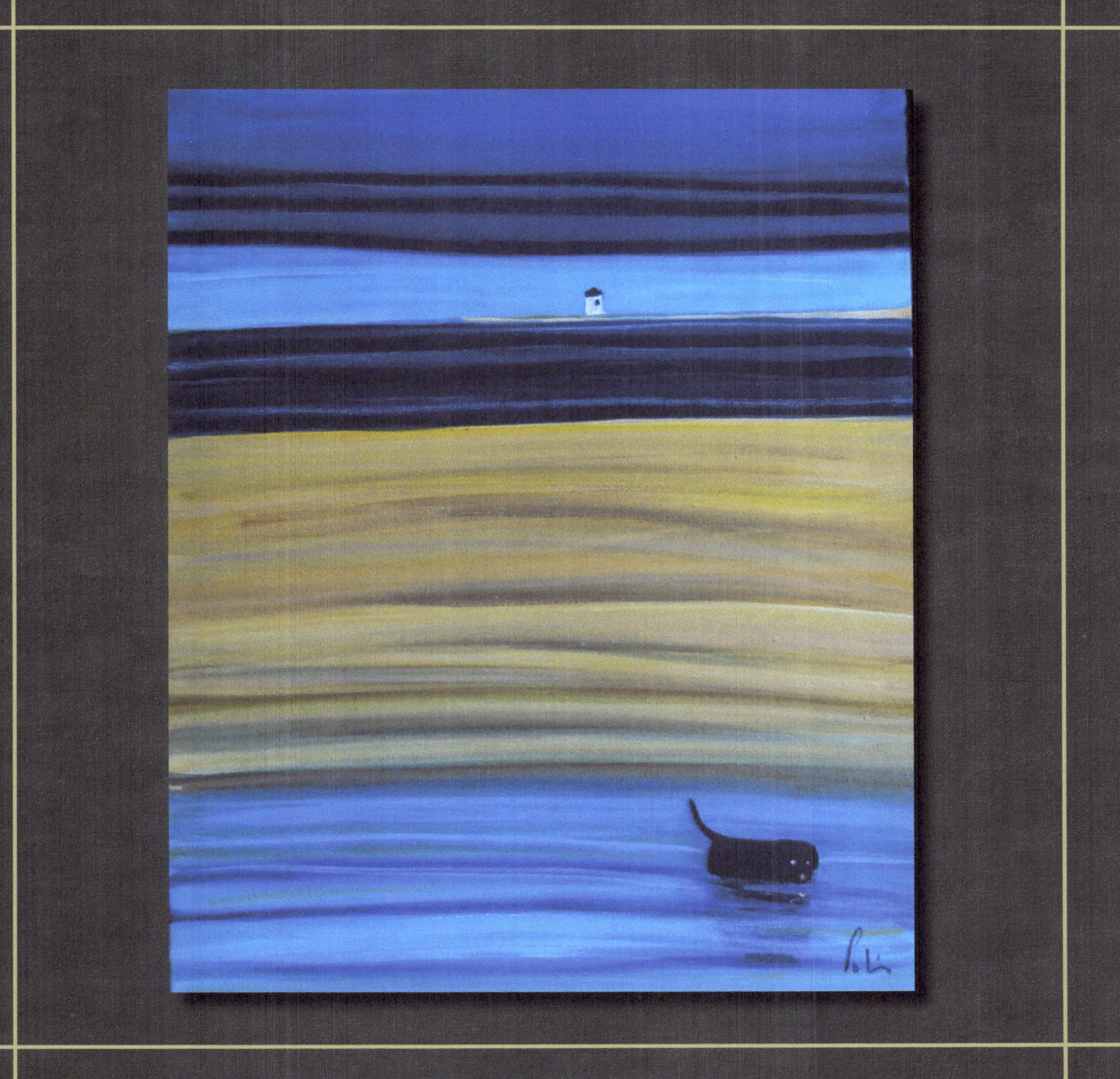

MICKEY AT THE RACE

"The Race Point lighthouse in the distance"

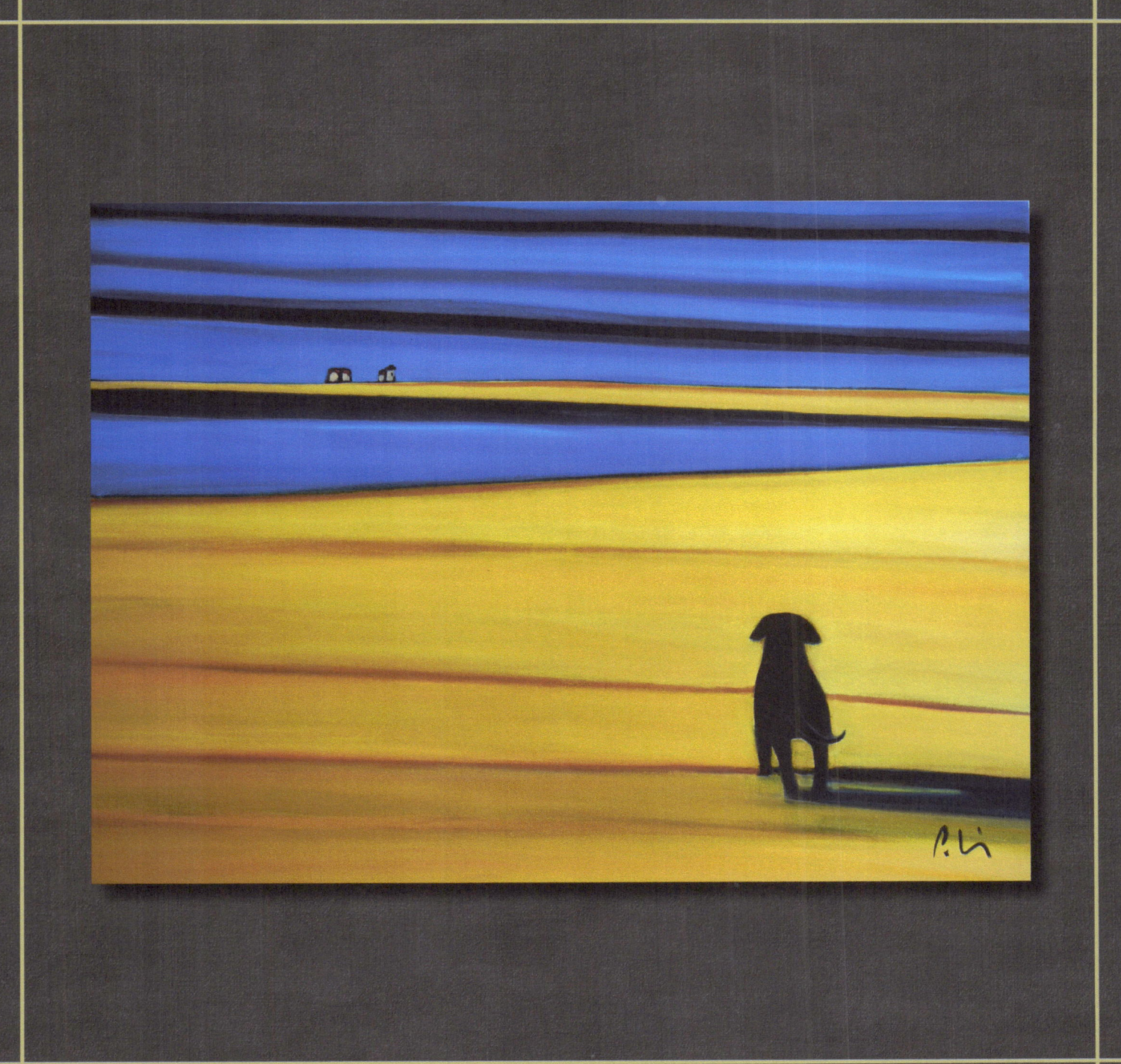

Moonshadow

"The shadow is the most important part of this painting."

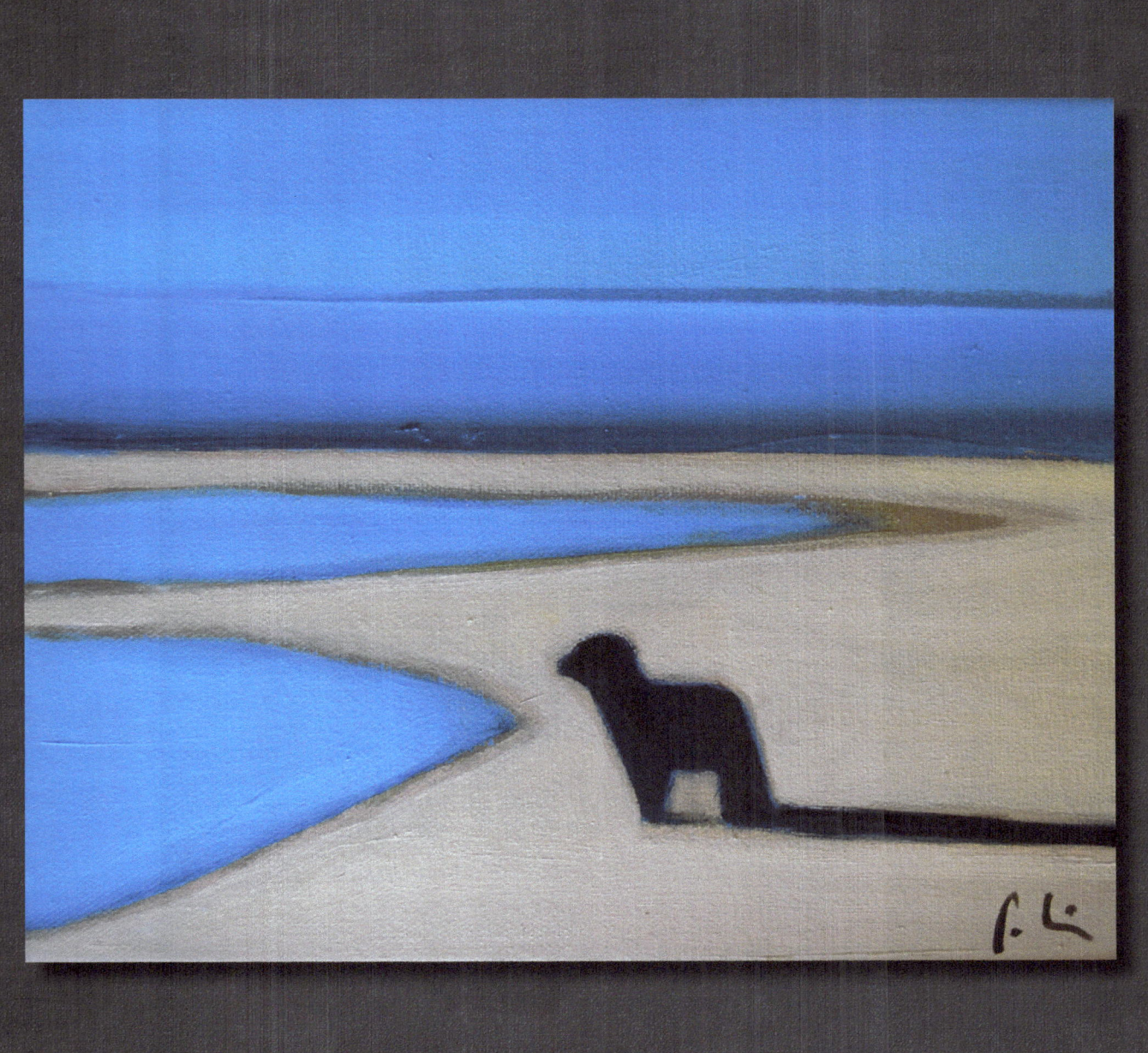

QUIET MOMENT

"So thoughtful."

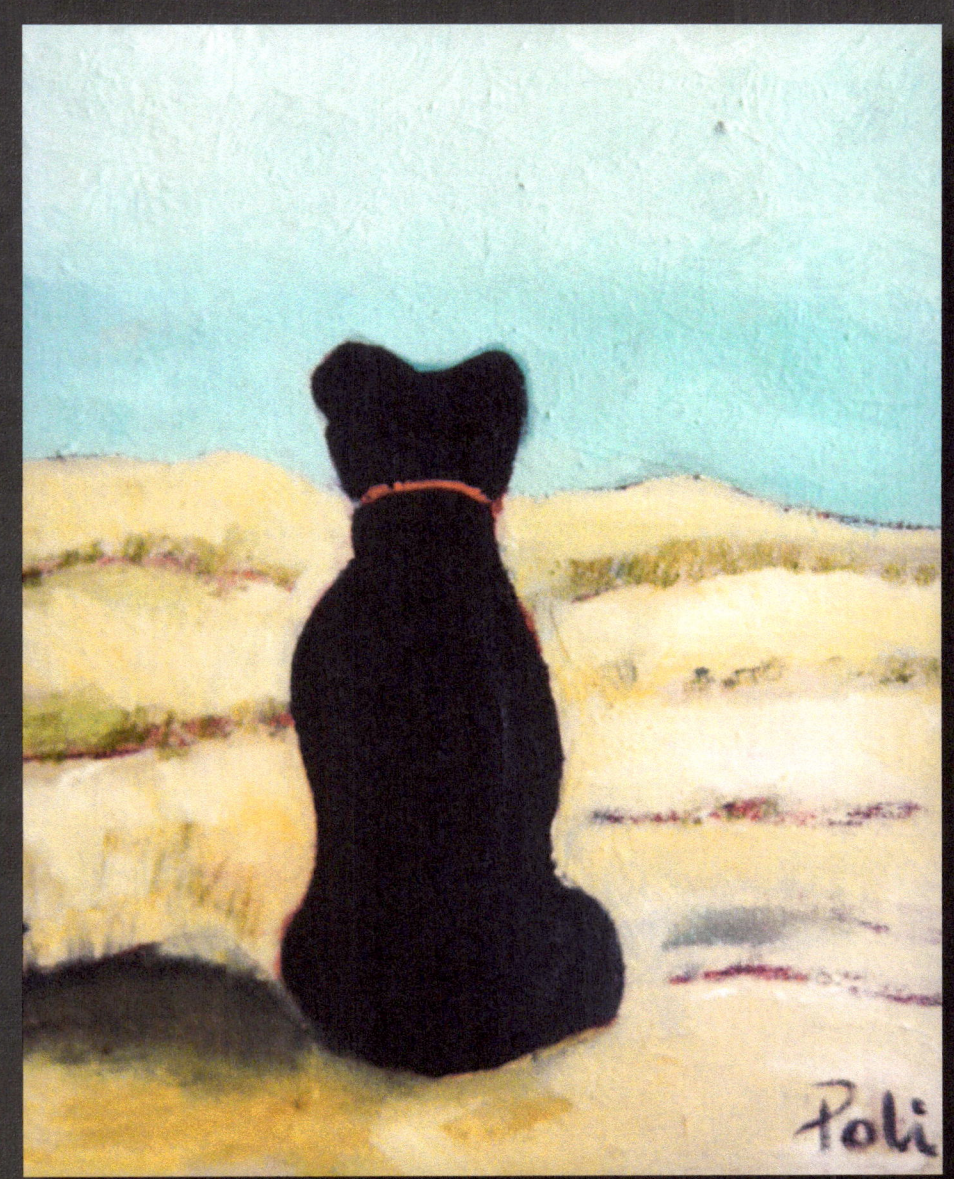

New Moon

"Through the trees."

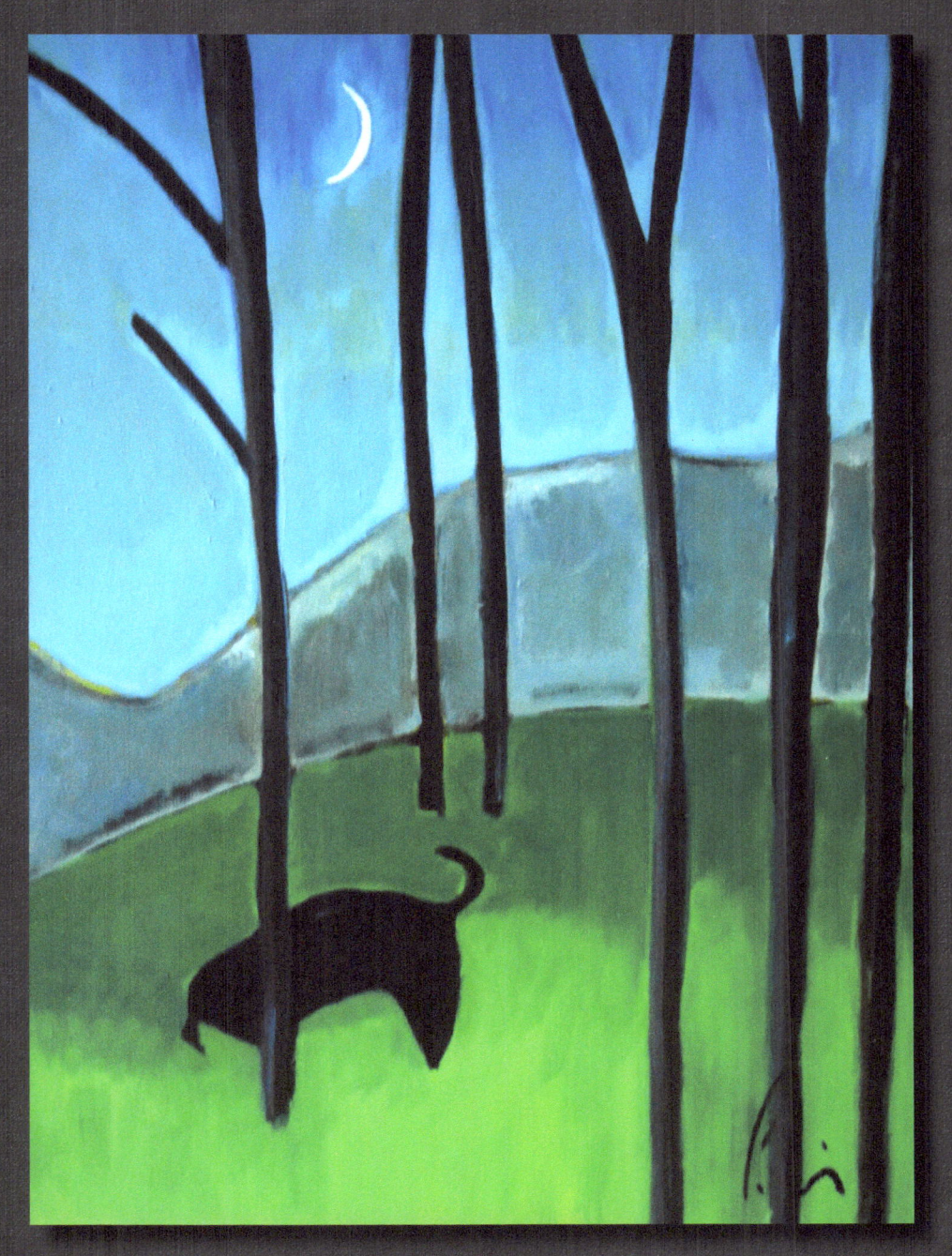

PABLITO

"A little painting of Pablo"

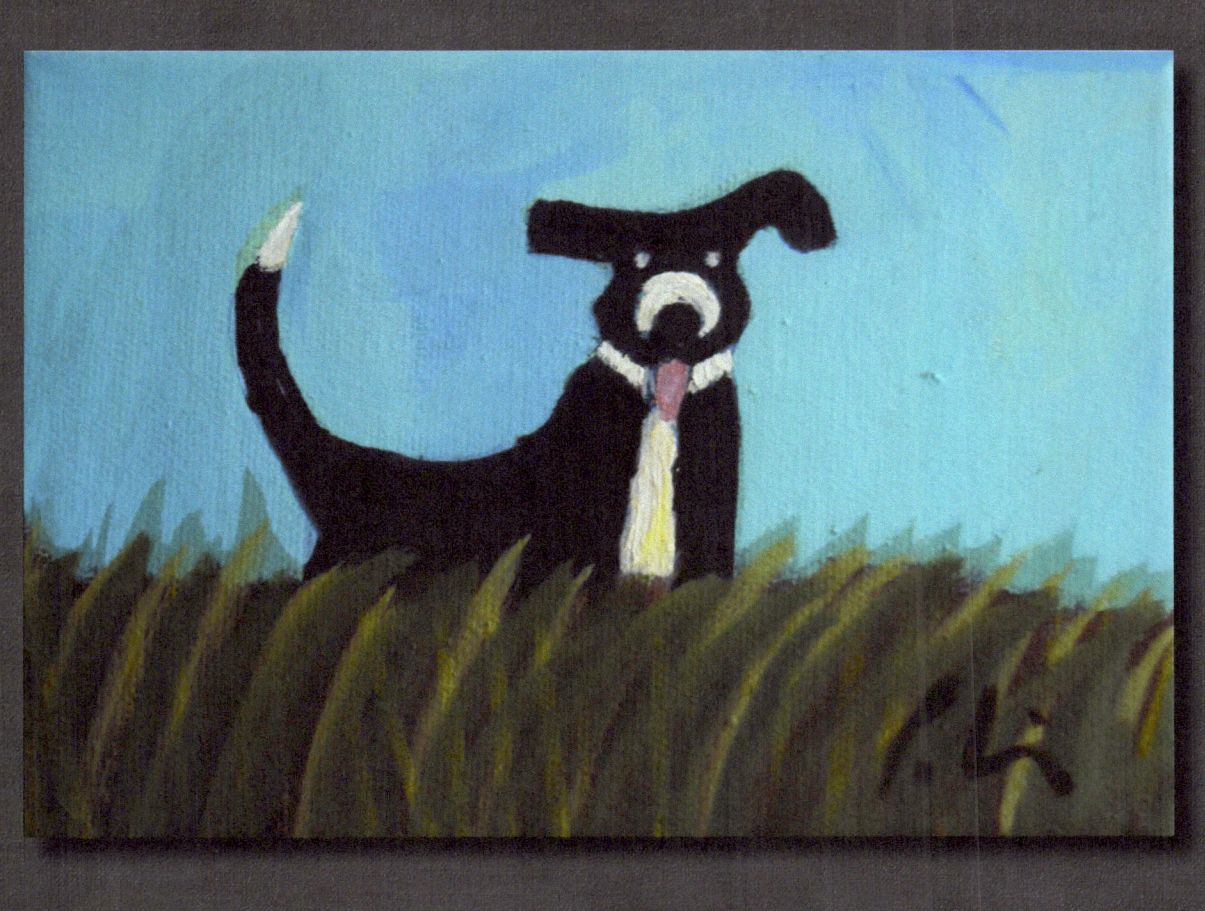

JOY

"There's no place he'd rather be."

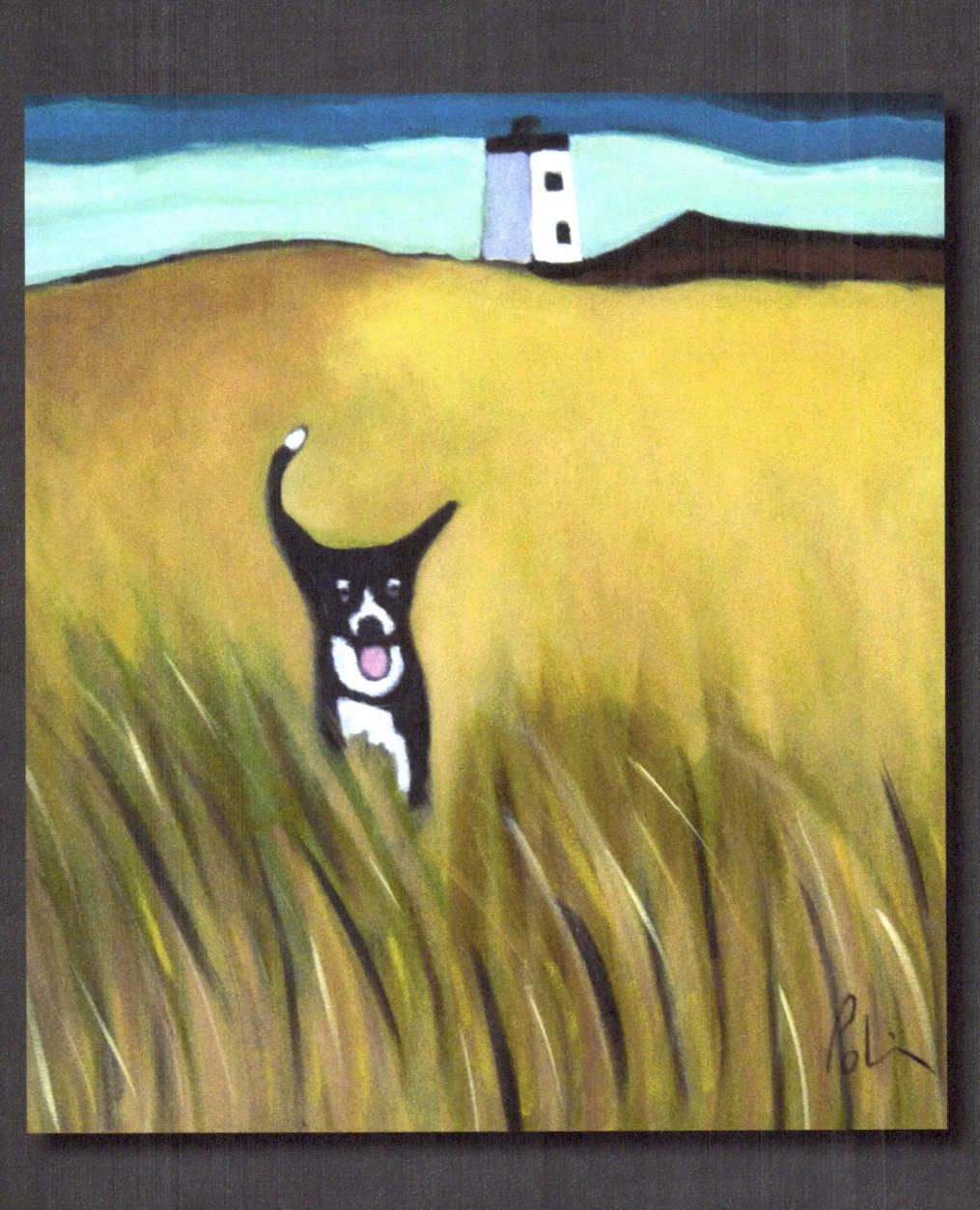

LUNA'S CHAIR

"Watching me cook—her favorite past time."

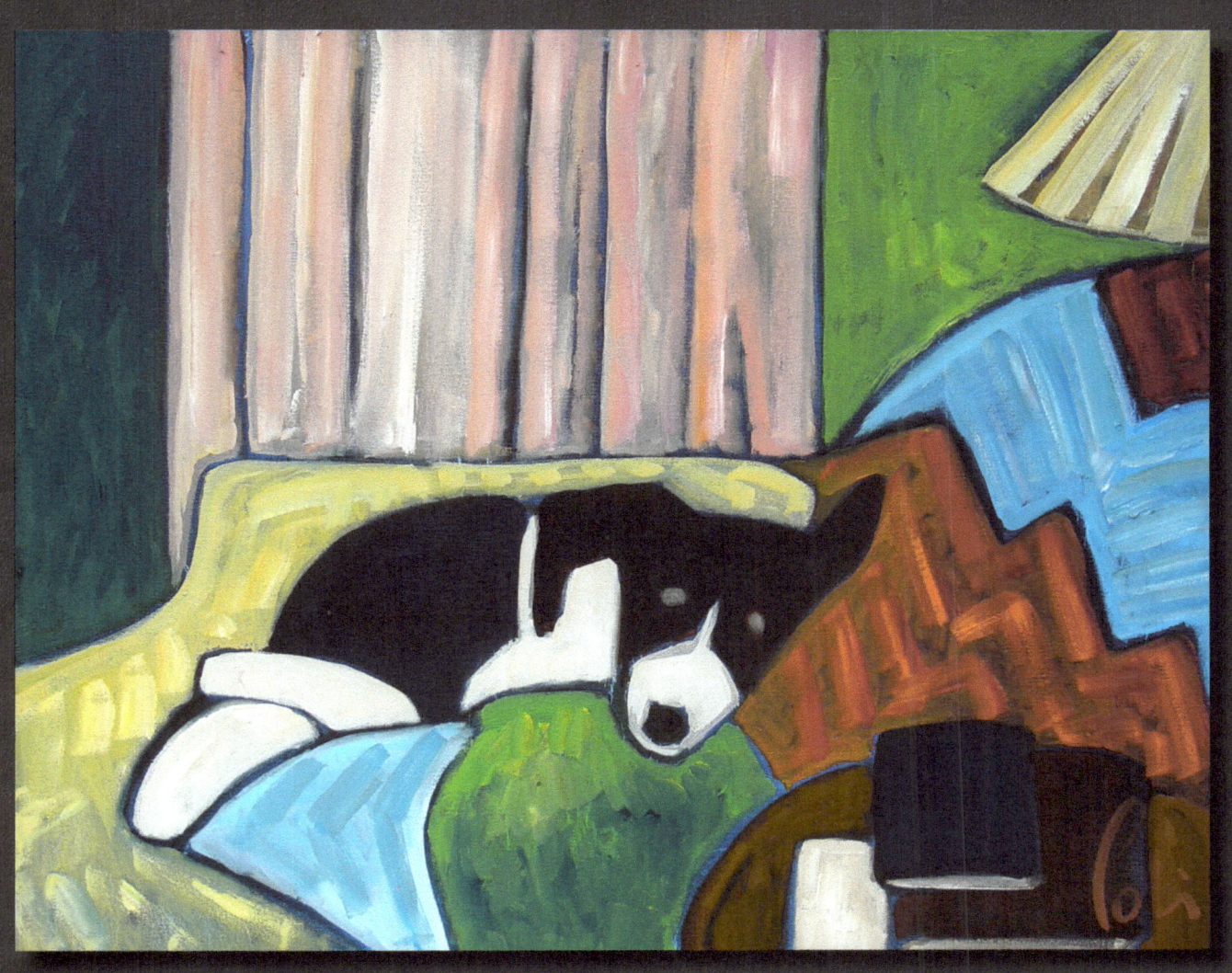

RUNNING THROUGH

"They love to play and hide."

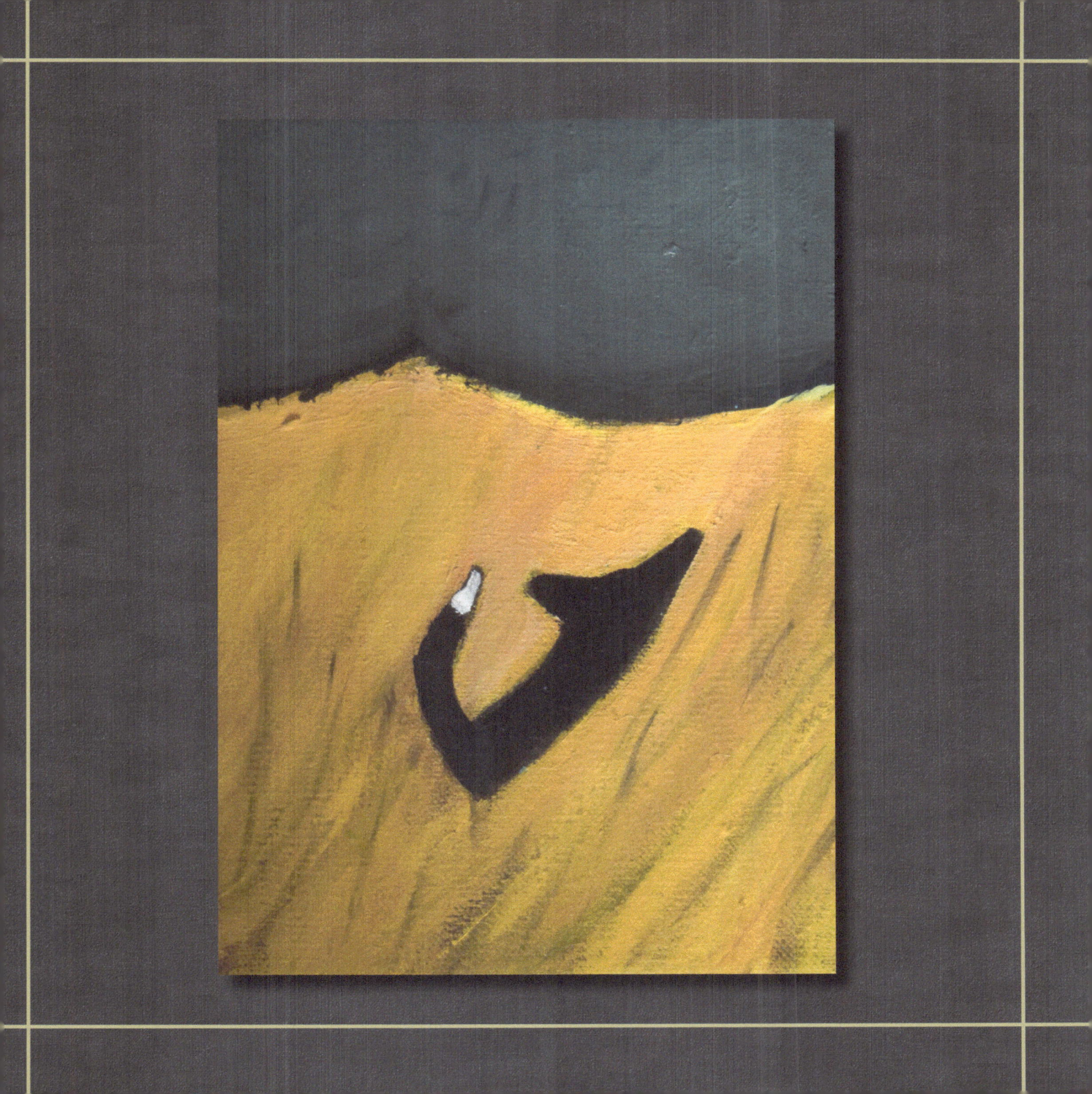

PROVINCETOWN MONUMENT

"Mickey's beautiful reflection"

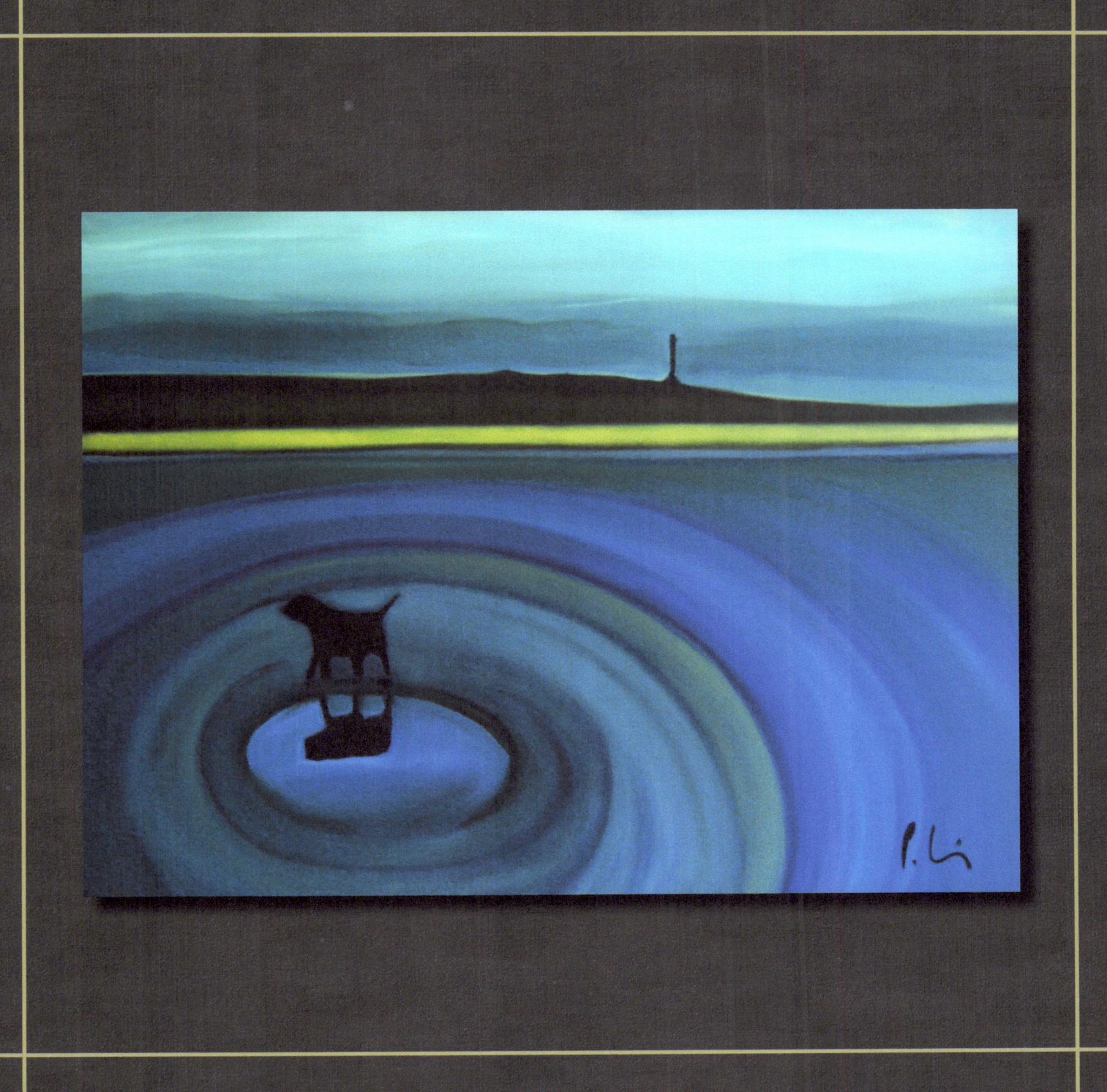

Reflection

"Foggy morning colors"

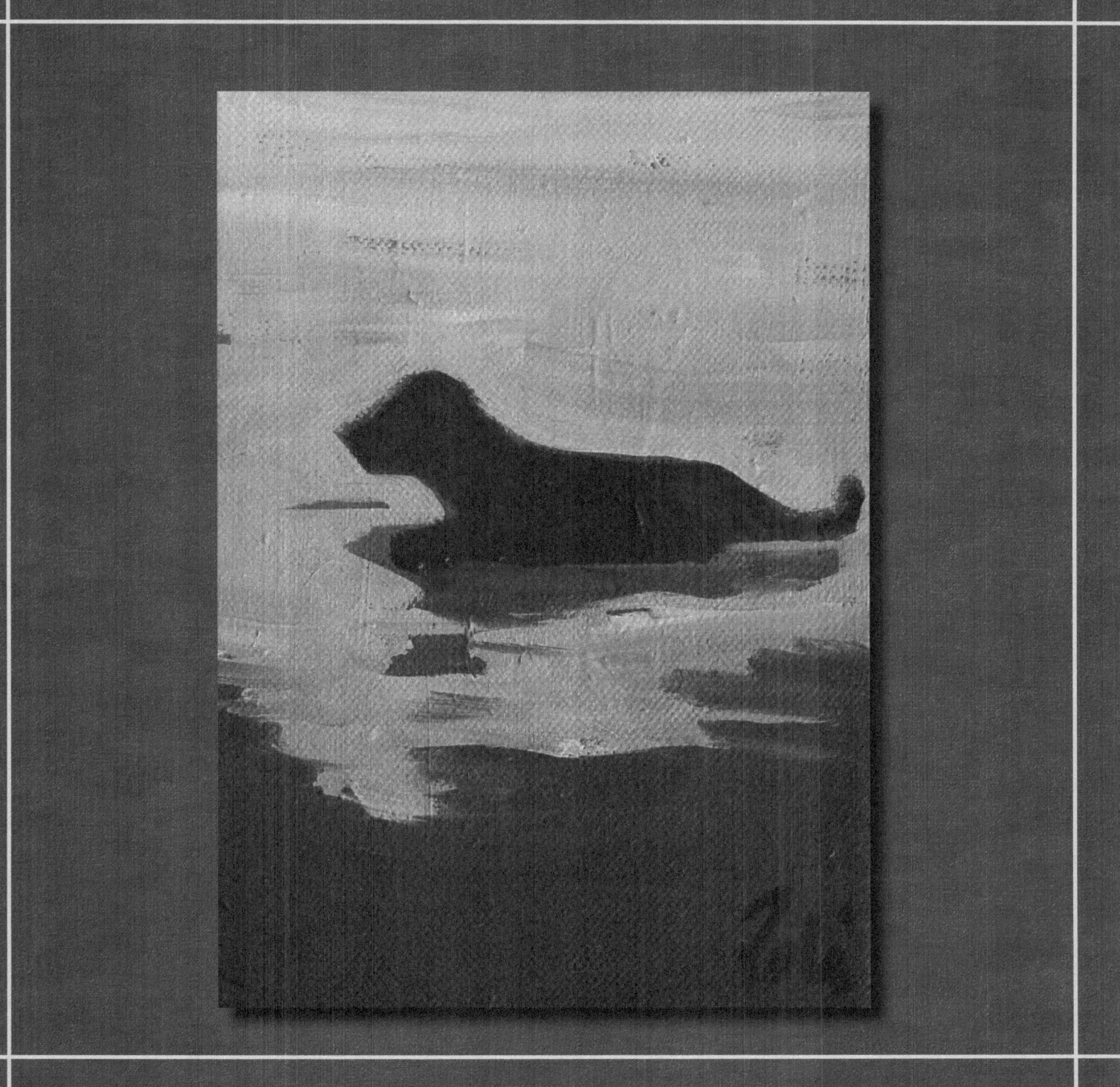

RUNNING

"His ears go up when he runs with a happy gait"

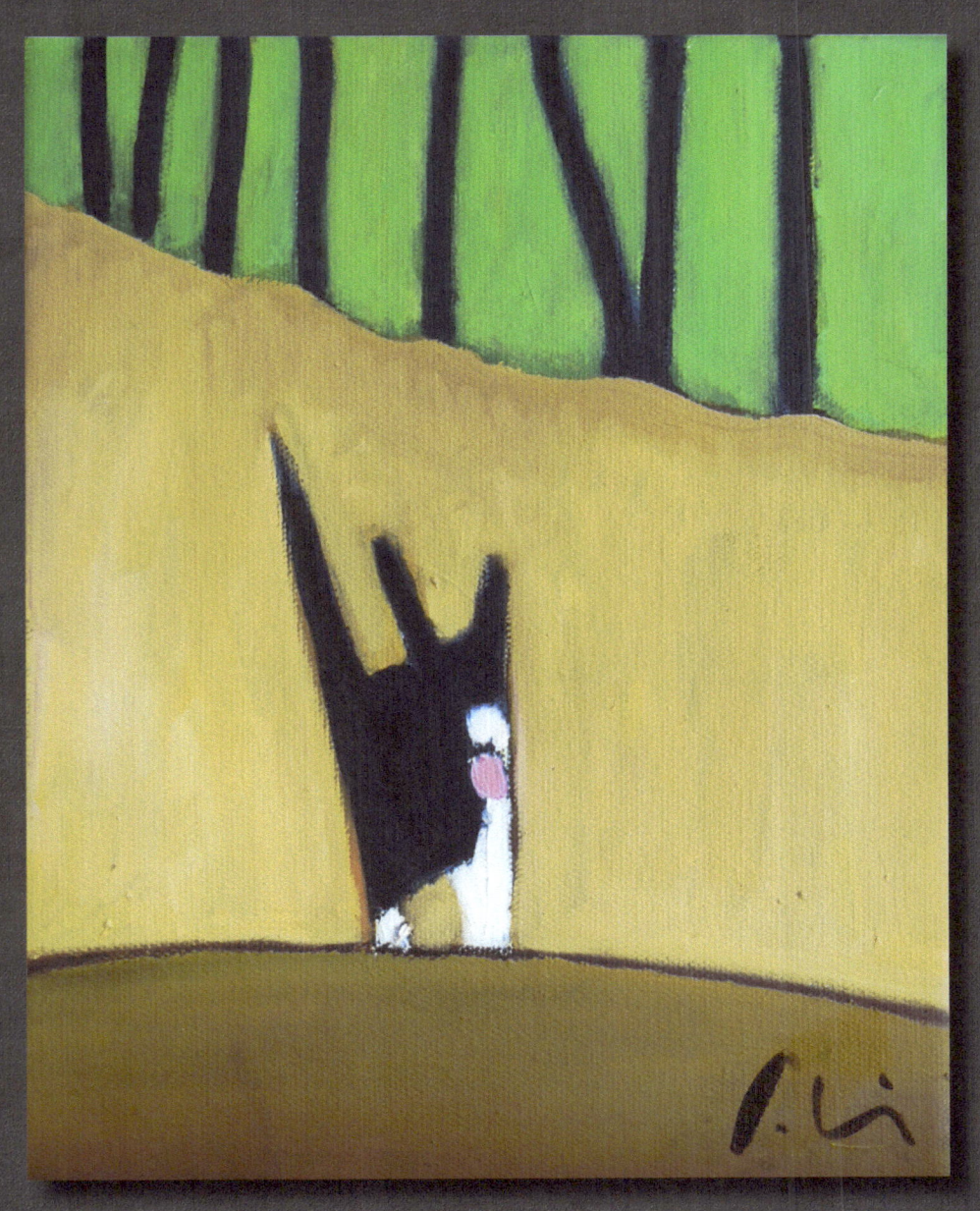

RUNNING AHEAD

"Galloping happliy through the woods"

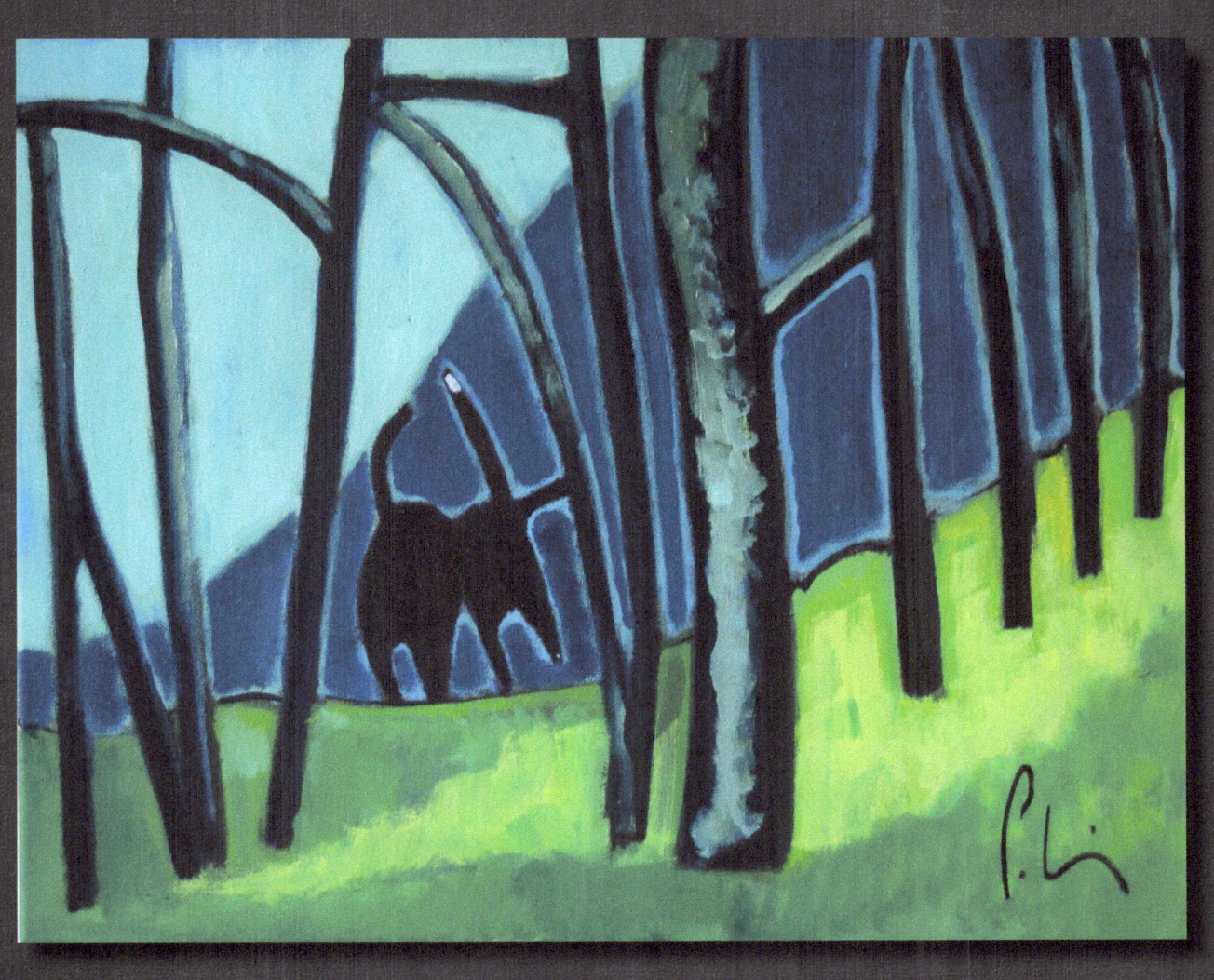

Shapes

"Mickey has the best silhouette"

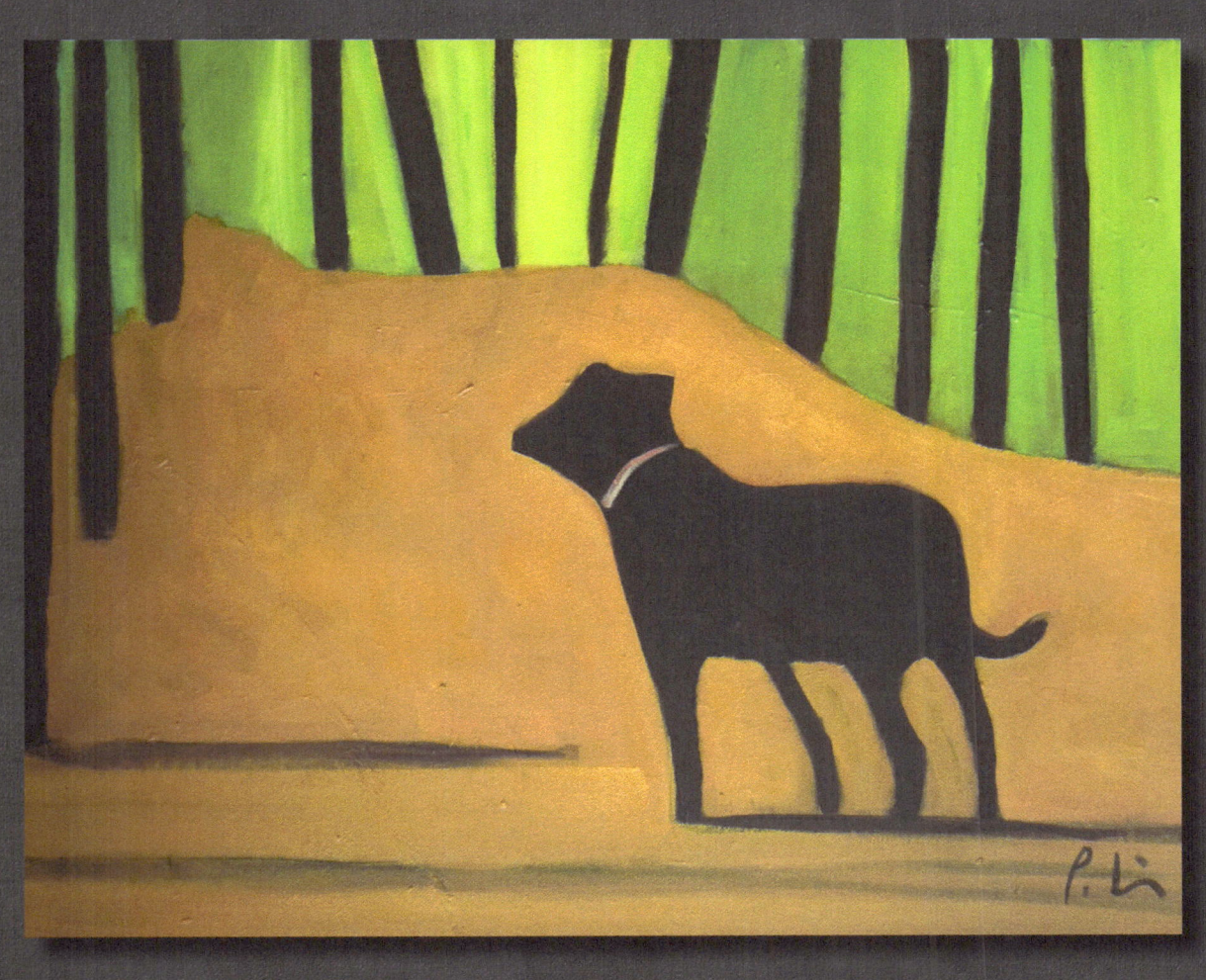

Sky

"Happy dog headed to the lighthouse"

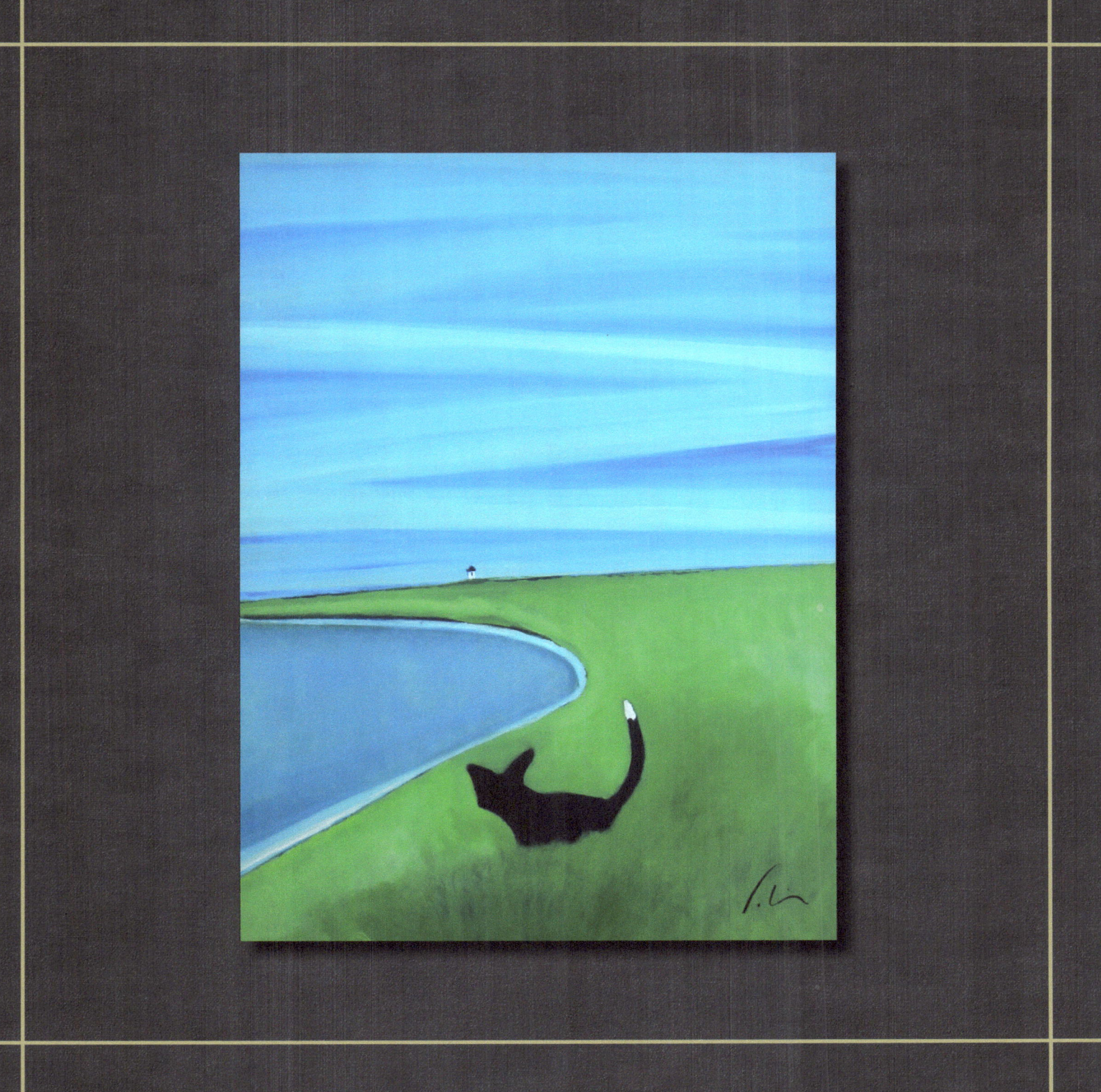

SIMPLE LINES

"Mickey is all black, nice and simple."

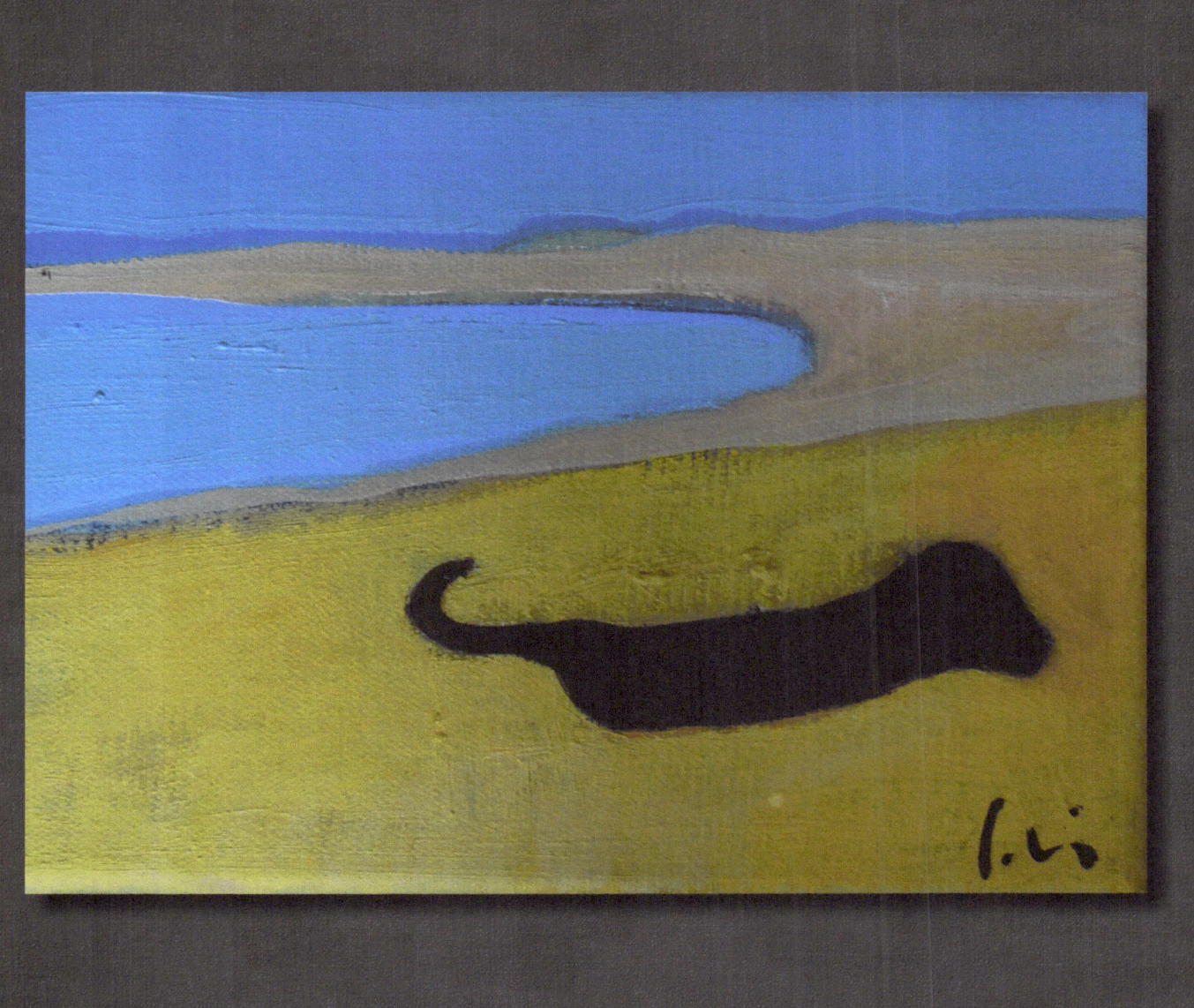

THE RACE
"Watching the seals"

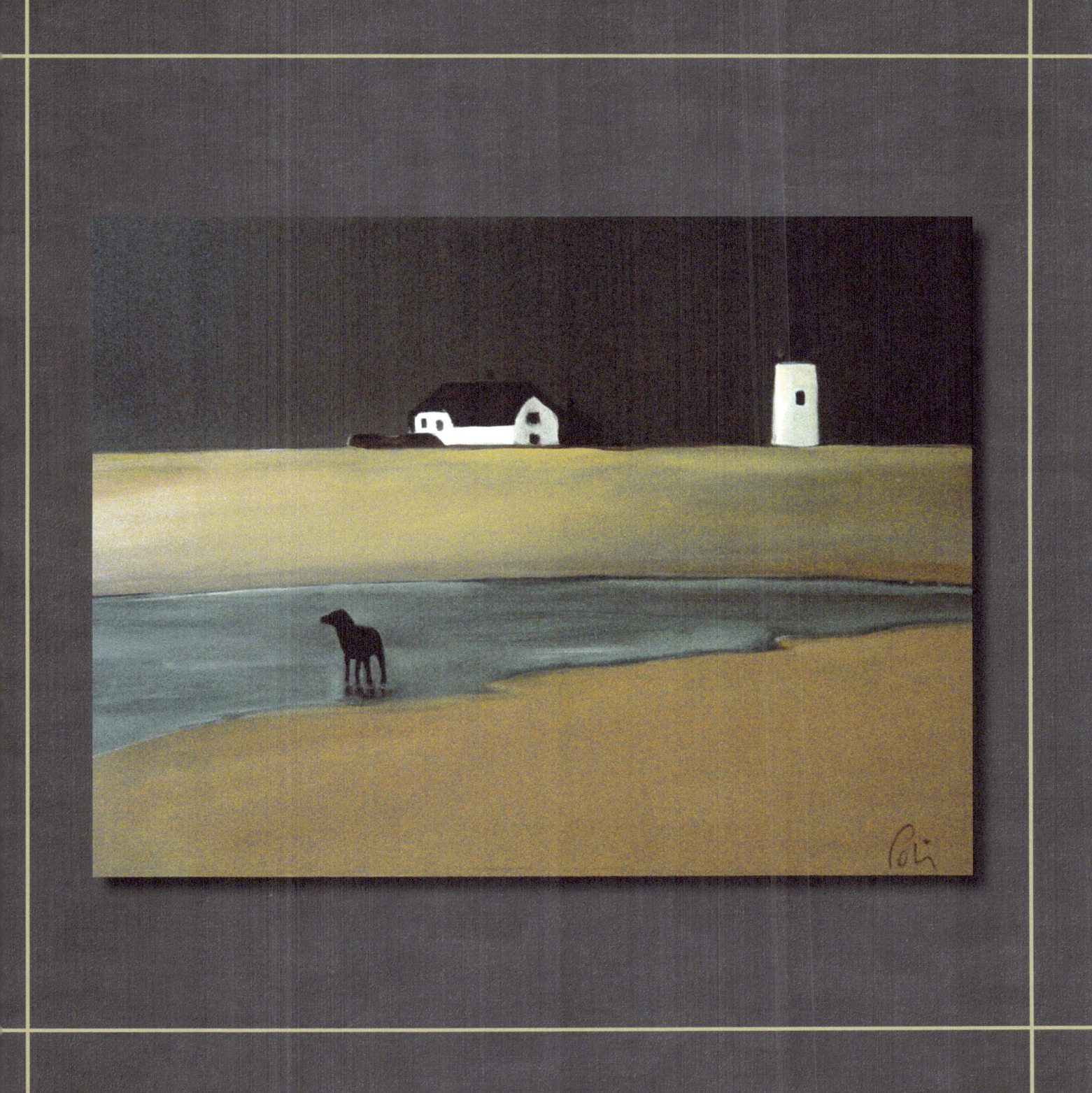

The Playground
"Pablo's favorite toy"

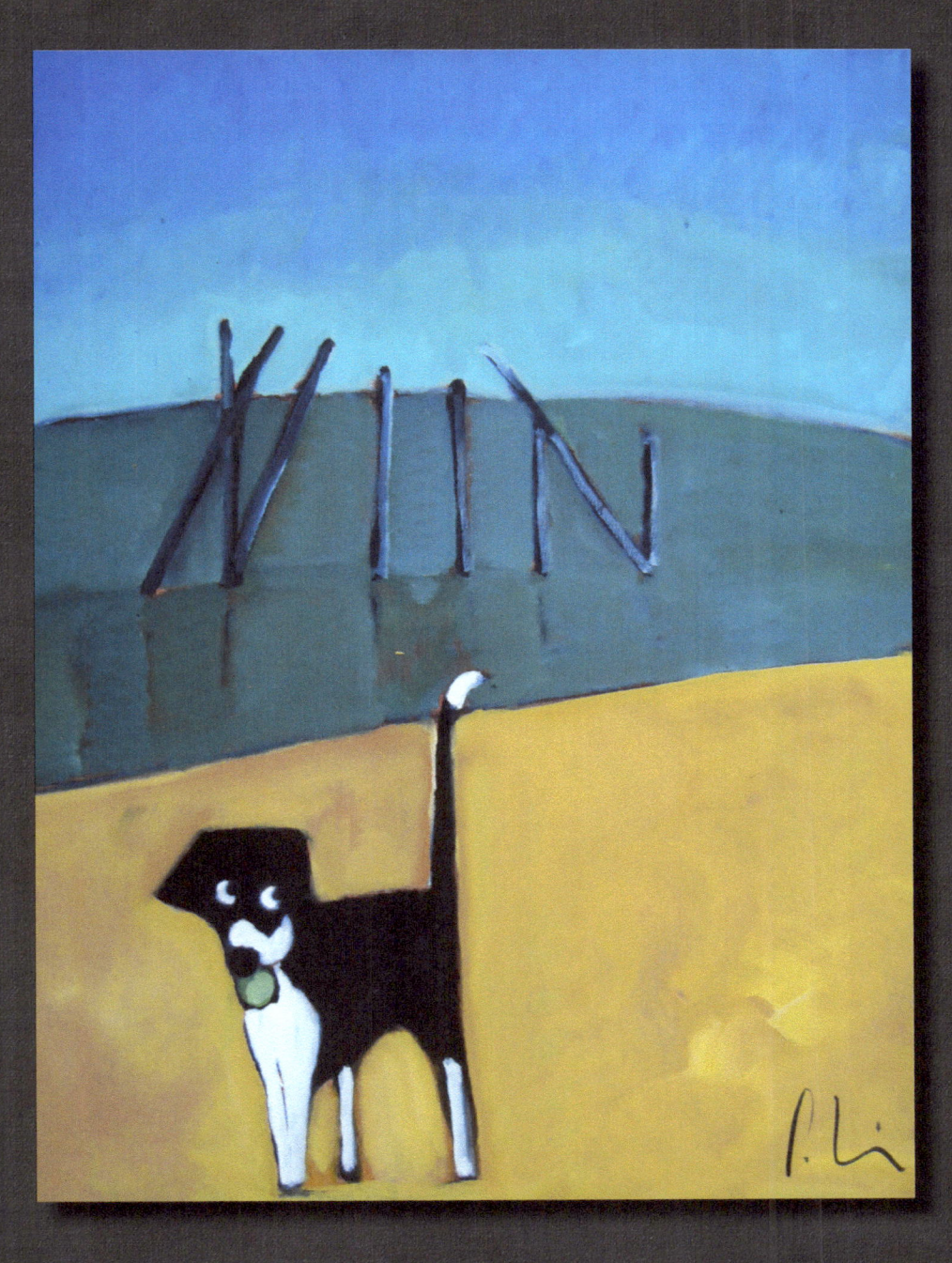

THE VAST HORIZON

"I love the shadow"

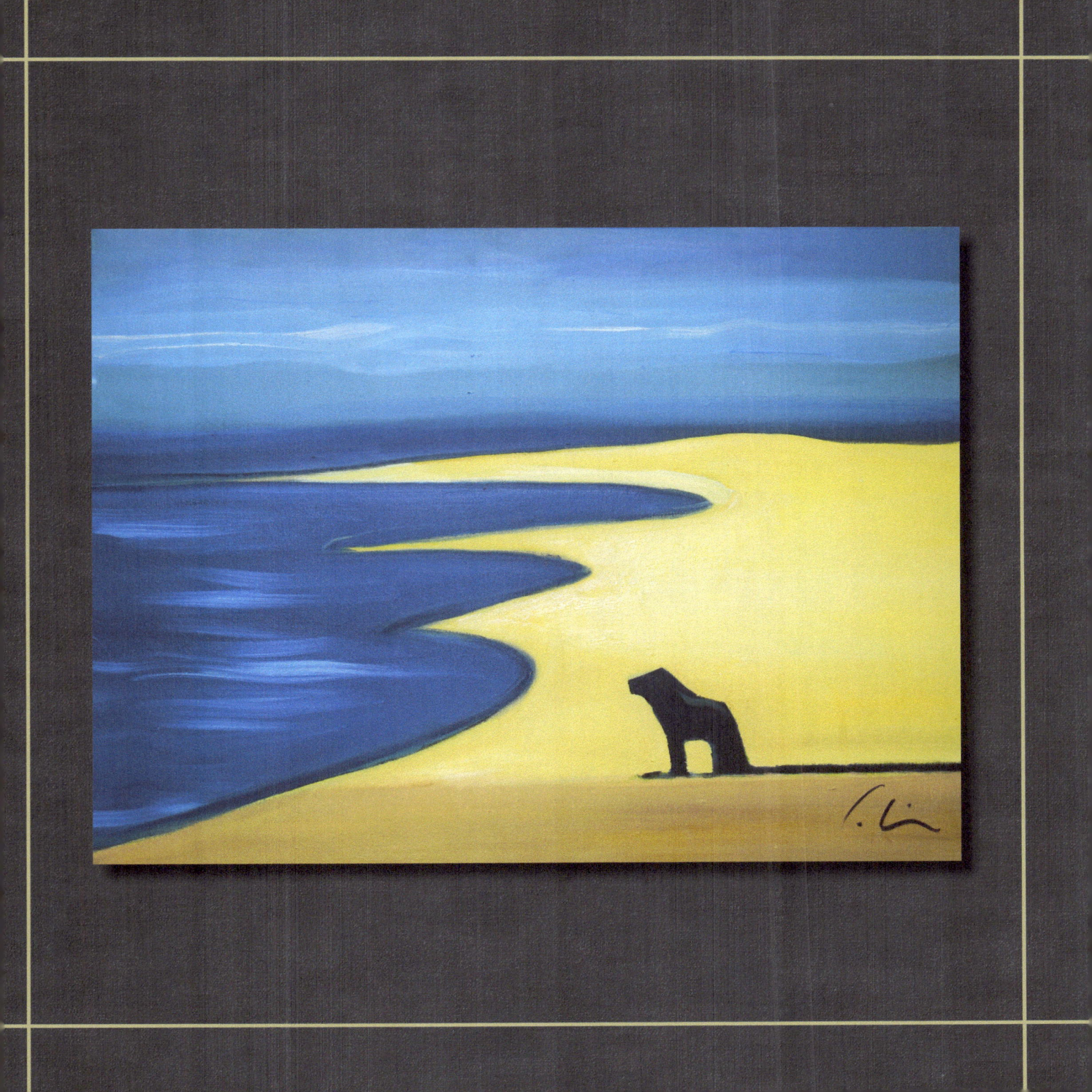

TIDE POOL

"The perfect time of day"

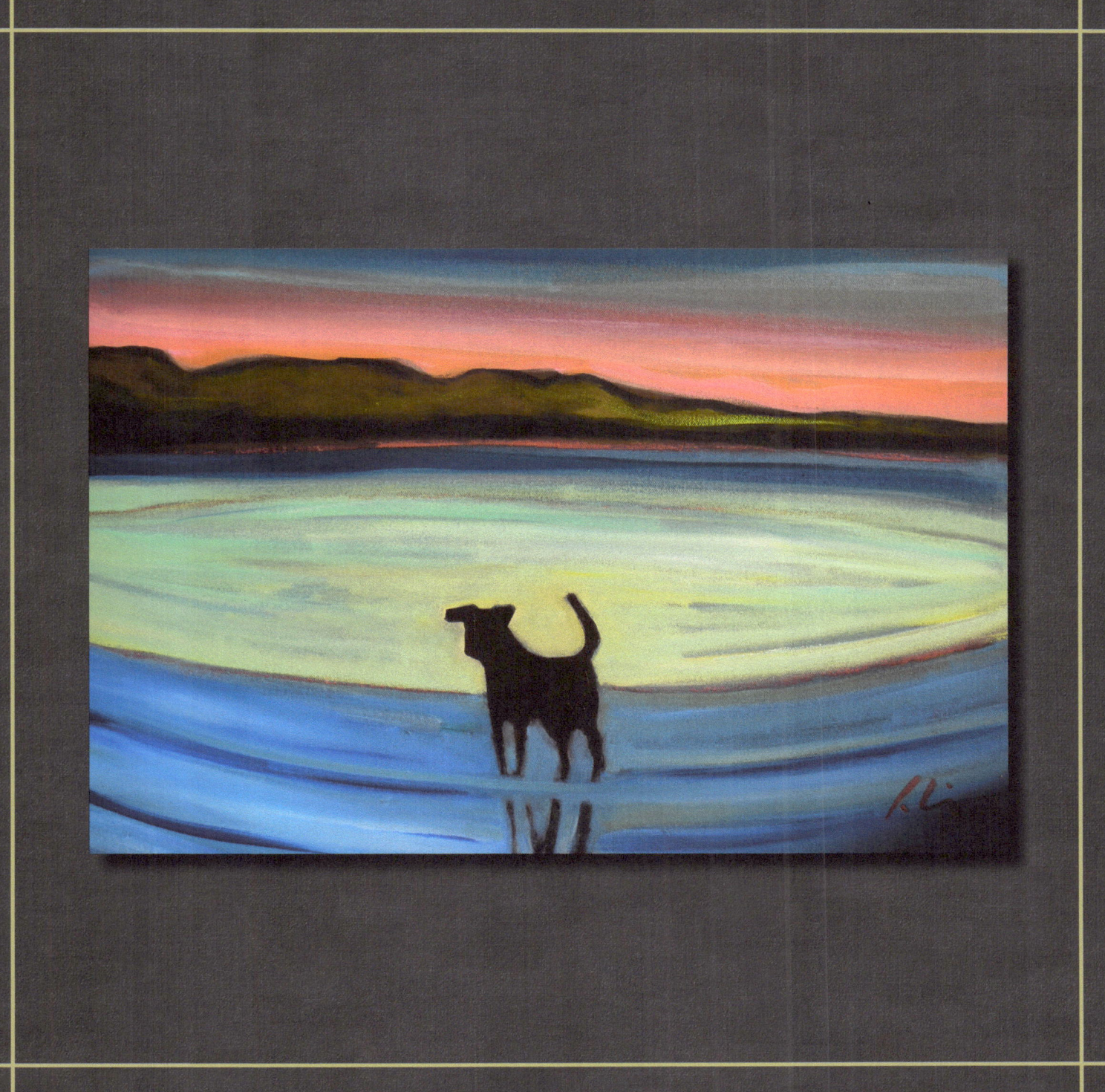

WEST

"So handsome in profile"

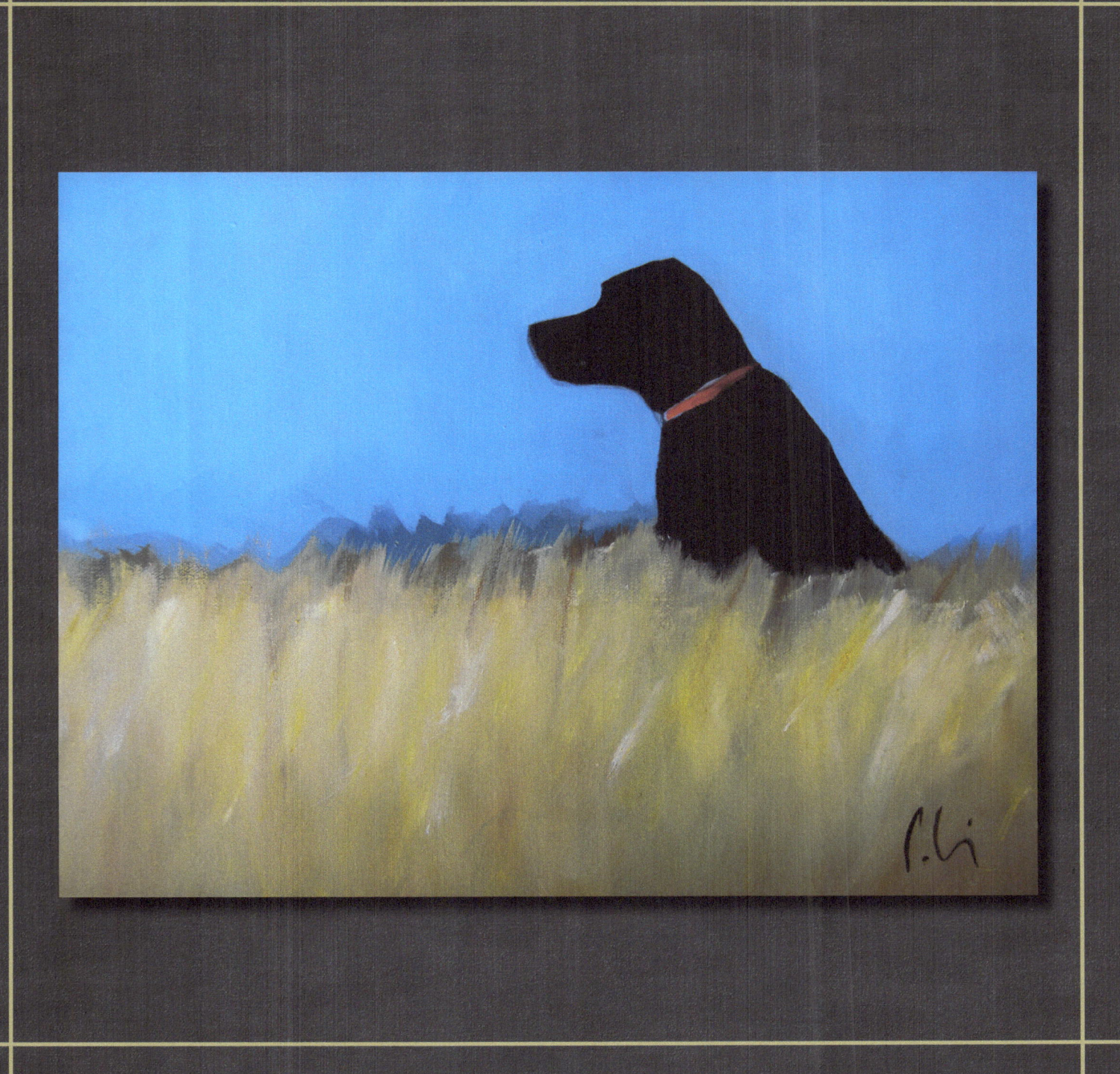

WIDE EYED AND BUSHY TAIL

"Headed towards the Wood End light house"

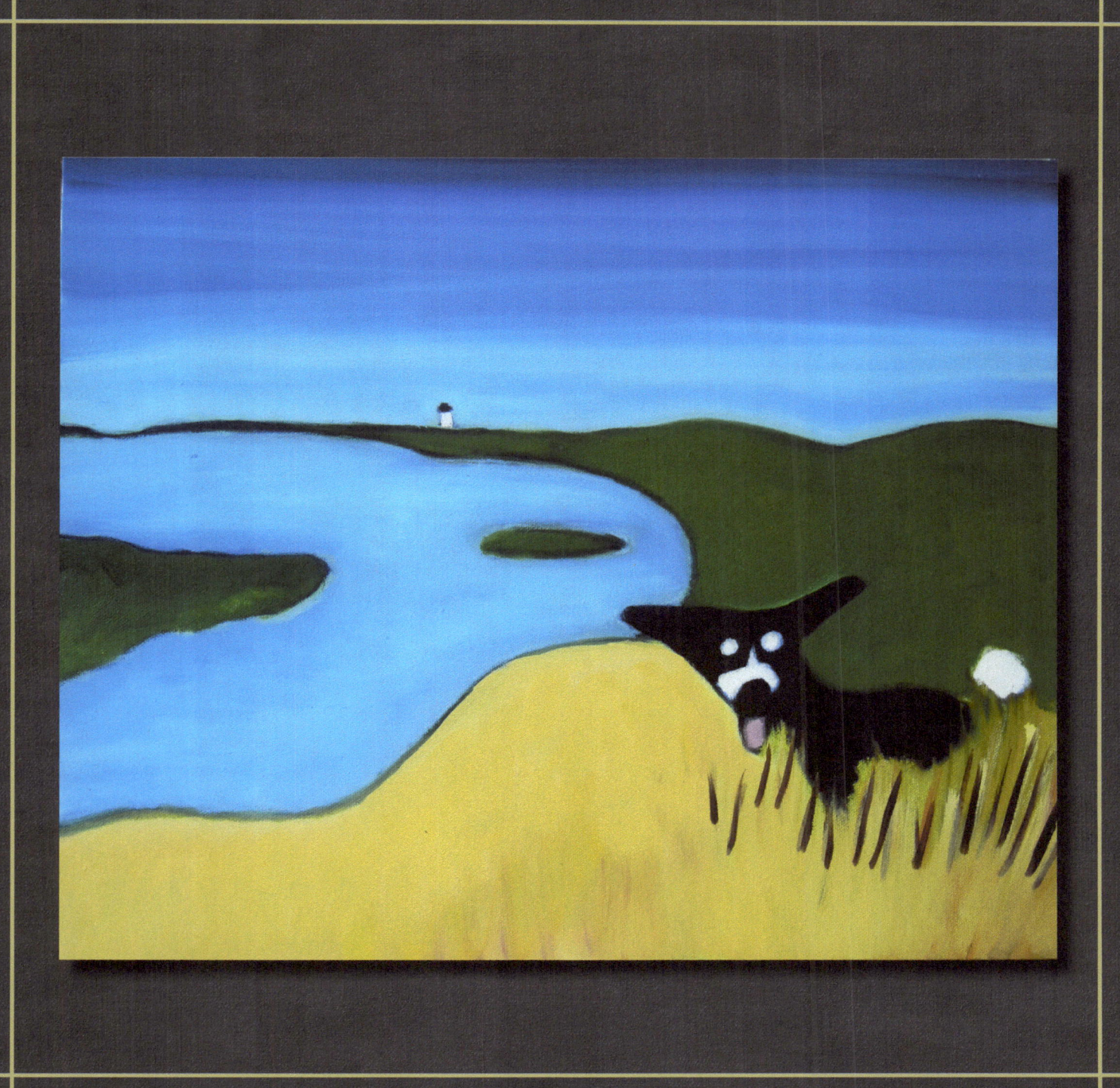

WOODS

"I'm using the least amount of detail to accentuate my dog's ears."

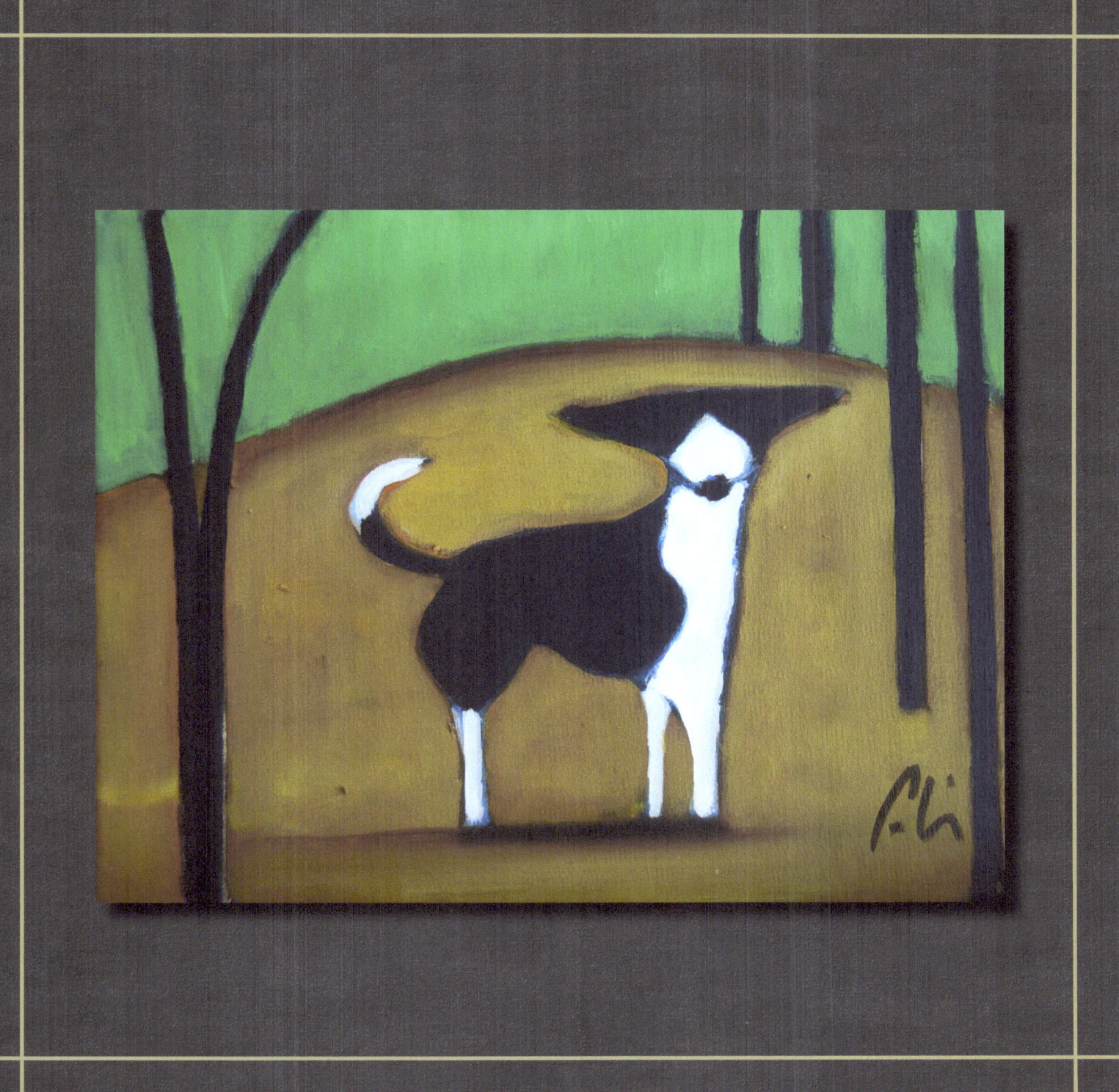

HER FAVORITE BED
"She LOVED this christmas gift."

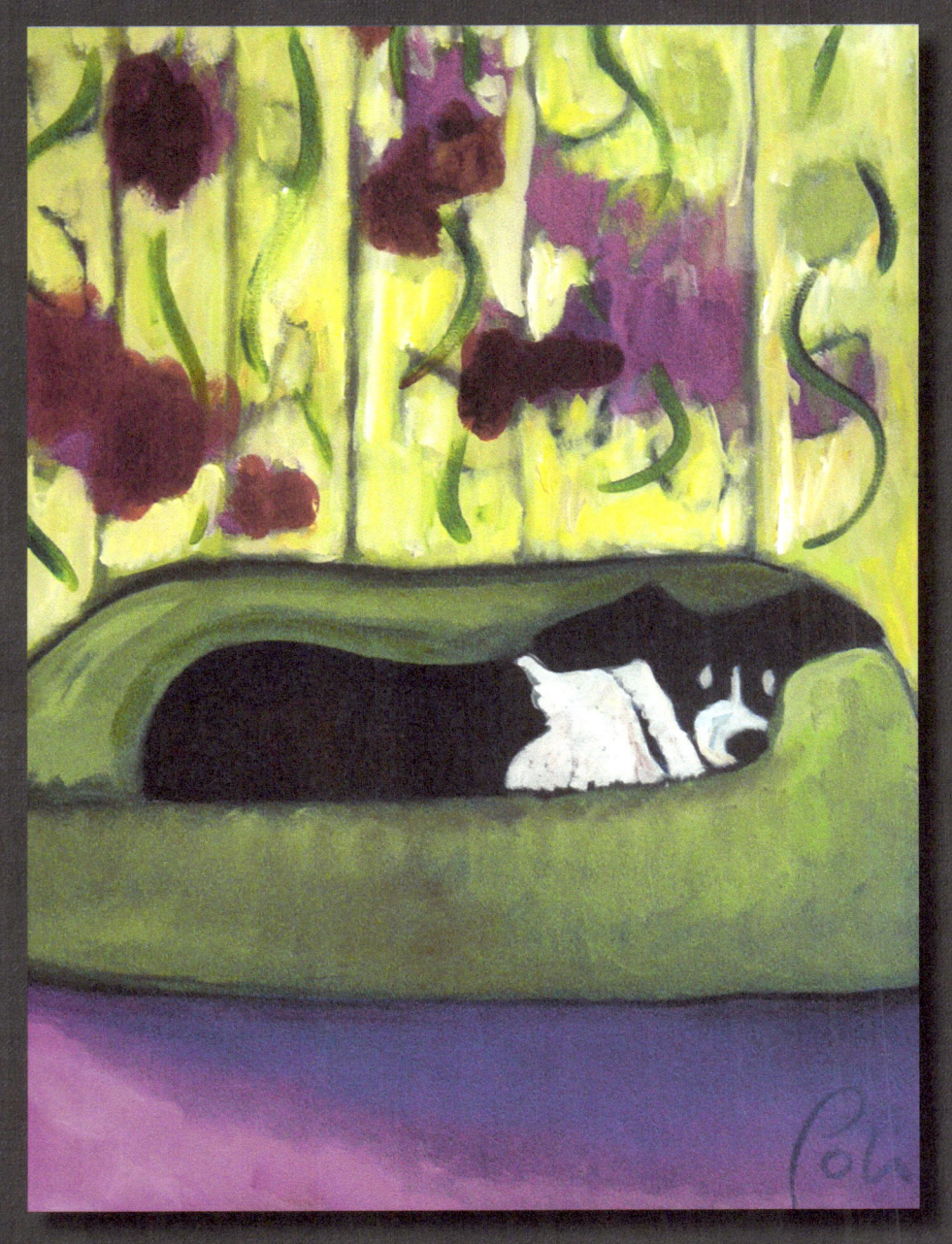

GREEN GRASS, PINK TONGUE

"He's smart and funny."

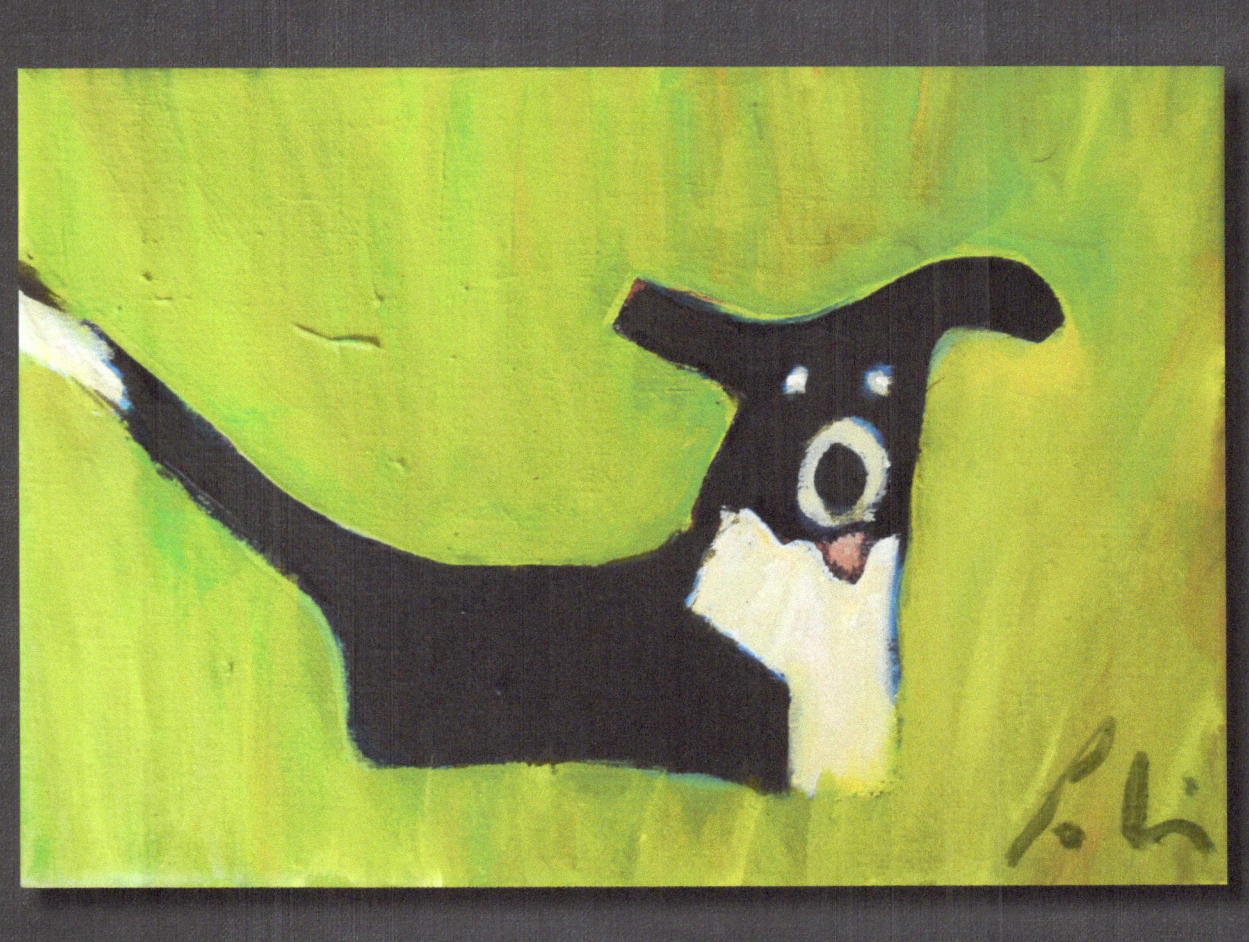

Two Dogs

"Side by side, true companions."

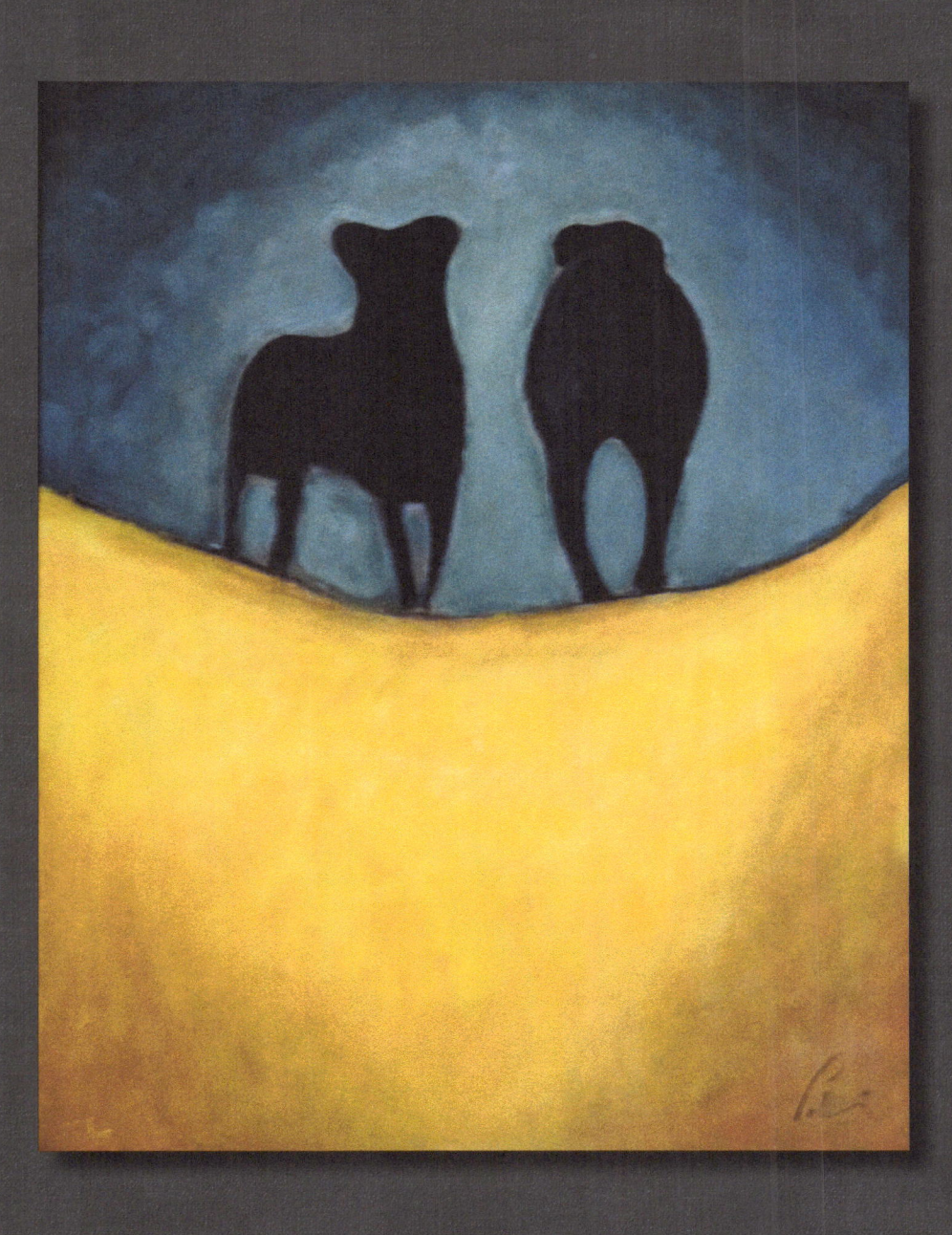

About The Artist

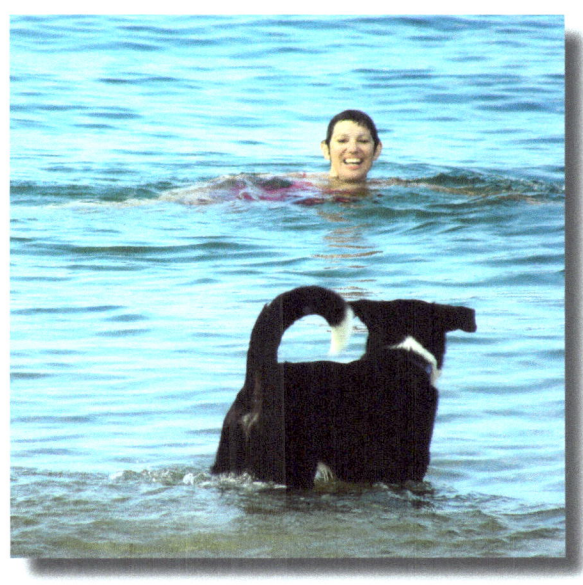

Nicoletta Poli was born in Hoboken, New Jersey, but moved to Molfetta, Italy at the age of three. She began drawing at a very young age and was inspired by her father, Paulo Poli, who was also a painter.

She returned to the United States with her family in 1968 and went on to graduate from the Fashion Institute of Technology in New York City. In 1982, during a visit to Provincetown, Cape Cod, she fell in love with the town and realized that there she could devote her life to her great love, painting. She immersed herself in the process of creating art, painting along with other artists and being inspired by the many well-known artist that have lived there.

As a self-taught artist, Poli approaches the canvas liberated from theories and doctrine. Immediately evident in her work are her bold choices of color and strong use of line. Poli is known for her elegant and whimsical canvases of animals, especially dogs. Her personal dogs were all rescued when she was living part-time in Tennessee in the 1990's. These dogs form the core of her work, and often generate commissioned work from customers wanting a painting of their own pet. "They give me great subject matter to paint and I can portray my love for them through my paintings," Poli says, "with a simple stoke and vivid color, I'm able to capture their true essence."

In 2000 Poli opened the Poli Gallery in Provincetown —"a dream come true."There she incorporates her dog paintings, still-lives and landscapes and accepts commissioned pet portraits. "As an animal lover it gives me great joy to paint not only my beautiful dogs and cat, but also beloved pets of others."

"When you paint a painting of a dog or cat, they come to life. Their memory and soul lives on."

For information about Poli's work and her commissions, call 508-487-5480 or visit:

POLi Gallery
349 Commercial St
Provincetown, MA

In addition to her original oil and watercolor paintings, the Poli Gallery also produces fine art Giclee' prints of select images. These prints utilize the finest museum quality inks and paper to produce an original affordable art work. They are available for order through:

POLIPAINTINGS.COM

Also, become a fan on the *POLi GALLERY* Facebook page.

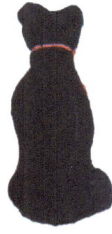

www.ingramcontent.com/pod-product-compliance
Lightning Source LLC
Chambersburg PA
CBHW050727180526
45159CB00003B/1151